PYTHON

For Absolute Beginners

**The Ultimate beginner's guide to Learn
Python Programming with Extensive Coverage
on Data Science and Web Programming**

OVER 200 PROGRAMMING
EXERCISES AND SOLUTIONS
INCLUDED

BONA AKUBUE

Nano✔dge

First published: February, 2024.
Published by NanoEdge Int'l Ltd
Lagos, Nigeria

Dedication

To my wife Stephanie and my children Ivy and Alexandra.

About the author

Bona Akubue is an experienced software developer with over 15 years of career experience. His expertise primarily revolves around Python development, a language he has mastered and utilized to revolutionize various projects and systems.

His journey in software development began with Visual Basic 6.0, marking his initial foray into programming. Motivated by curiosity and commitment, he delved into mastering various programming languages like Visual Basic.NET, Java, and C#, enriching his technical skills.

However, it was the allure of Python that captured his imagination, eventually becoming his primary focus due to its flexibility, readability, and powerful capabilities.

Beyond his professional achievements, Bona's enthusiasm for software engineering extends to sharing his knowledge and expertise with aspiring developers. He actively engages in mentoring and educating others, empowering the next generation of tech enthusiasts to navigate the intricate world of programming with confidence and skill.

Driven by a desire to push the boundaries of innovation and create solutions that make a tangible difference, Bona Akubue continues to make indelible contributions to the tech industry, inspiring others through his expertise, entrepreneurial spirit, and unwavering dedication to technological excellence.

Acknowledgments

Writing a book on Python programming has been an incredible journey filled with challenges and triumphs, and it wouldn't have been possible without the support and encouragement of numerous individuals. I am deeply grateful to everyone who contributed to this endeavor.

I extend my heartfelt gratitude to my family for their unwavering support and understanding throughout the countless hours spent researching, writing, and revising. Your patience and encouragement fueled my determination to see this project through.

I am indebted to the Python community for their vibrant discussions, shared knowledge, and endless enthusiasm for this remarkable programming language. Your collective passion has been a constant source of inspiration.

I extend my thanks to the editorial and publishing team whose dedication and hard work transformed my manuscript into a polished book. Your professionalism and attention to detail have been instrumental in bringing this project to fruition.

I am immensely grateful to all the reviewers and editors whose feedback and suggestions played a crucial role in refining the content and ensuring its accuracy and relevance.

Lastly, to the readers—thank you for your interest in Python programming. It is my sincere hope that this book serves as a valuable resource in your journey to explore, learn, and master Python.

Thank you to everyone who supported me on this rewarding Journey.

Preface

Learning Python was quite a challenge for me, to be honest. Back in the day, there were two versions to choose from: Python 2 and Python 3, and I struggled with deciding which one to go for. While I was grappling with the version dilemma, I also faced difficulties finding the right learning materials to guide me through the process.

Most of the books I came across were either not comprehensive enough or simply hard to comprehend. Some were overly lengthy, filled with unnecessary details, and difficult to follow. Others lacked sufficient examples and exercises for practice.

Sure, the official documentation was helpful, but it wasn't comprehensive enough and lacked real-world examples. I scoured countless books, documentation, and online blogs in my pursuit of Python knowledge.

Although I stumbled upon a few helpful books, I still felt there was a need for more.

I always wished for a single book that would guide a novice like me from start to finish without having to seek additional resources.

Today, I am glad to present to you that book.

My goal is to help you reduce your learning curve by giving you a book that is not only easy to understand but beginner-focused.

This book is written in a clear and concise style, with plenty of examples and exercises to help you practice your new skills. So many practical tips and tricks were included throughout the book to help you avoid common pitfalls and write clean and efficient code.

This book covers all the fundamental concepts of Python programming such as data types, variables, control structures, functions, and modules. Also, more advanced topics like object-oriented programming, file handling and asynchronous programming were also covered.

Now, if you're still wondering whether Python is a good choice, especially if you're new to programming, let me assure you that it absolutely is!

Python is a powerful and versatile language with a wide range of applications, from web development and data analysis to scientific computing and artificial intelligence.

Who is this book for?

If you've never programmed before and want to start programming in Python, you've made an excellent choice. Whether you're interested in pursuing a career in programming or just want to learn a valuable new skill, this book is the perfect starting point.

How to use this book

The truth is, learning programming can be overwhelming, and many people lose interest along the way. Like any other profession, programming requires a serious level of commitment.

To get the most out of this book, my advice is not to skip any part of it. Although the chapters are independent, if you're a complete beginner, I recommend reading them sequentially. However, if you're an experienced programmer looking to refresh your memory, feel free to jump to any chapter that piques your interest.

Programming is a practical subject and not something you can memorize or read like the novel. So, code along as you read the book.

Many times, you might think you understand something, only to draw a blank when asked to put it into practice. By typing in the code examples on your own computer, you'll solidify your understanding and avoid any false sense of familiarity.

So, punch in every code you see or read on your computer.

There are lots of examples and exercises that will help you master the topics. I encourage you to try out all the exercises by yourself to enable you build confidence in yourself.

I encourage you to tackle all the exercises on your own to build confidence in your abilities. However, if you find yourself struggling with a particular problem, feel free to consult the solutions available on the book's website or GitHub repository.

By the time you reach the end of this book, you'll have gained sufficient skills to tackle real-world problems.

Conventions

In this book, you will find a number of styles of text that distinguish between different kinds of information. Here are some examples of these styles, and an explanation of their meaning.

Terminal commands follow the UNIX format and the dollar ($) sign is not part of the command:

$ python3 --version

A block of code is set as follows:

```
if num % 2 == 0:
    print("This is an even number.")
```

Important notes and coding tips appear in as follows:

> **Pro Tip**
> *This is an important information.*

Source codes

The source code for this book and solutions for exercises are available at https://bonaakubue.com/downloads. Also, you can find the GitHub repository accompanying this book through this link.

Bonus materials

This book comes with free bonus materials and cheats sheets. You can access these resources through https://bonaakubue.com/downloads.

Questions

While you're reading this book, if you have any questions, don't hesitate to reach out via email at python-book-questions@bonaakubue.com. I'm here to help, and I'll make sure to respond promptly to your inquiries. Additionally, I encourage you to sign up for my free newsletter at https://bonaakubue.com/subscribe. By subscribing, you'll gain access to programming tips, insightful articles, and updates on this book. It's a great way to stay connected and further enhance your programming journey.

Reader feedback

Your feedback is incredibly valuable for the ongoing improvement of this book. I genuinely want to hear your thoughts, whether it's about what you enjoyed or any areas you felt could be enhanced. Please don't hesitate to reach out by sending an feedback@bonaakubue.com, and kindly mention the book title in the subject line of your message. Your input will be greatly appreciated as I strive to make this book even better.

Errata

Great care has been taken to ensure the accuracy of this book. However, if you happen to come across any errors, whether in the text or the code, please help us by notifying us via email at python-book-errata@bonaakubue.com. Your attention to detail and assistance in identifying any mistakes will be highly appreciated.

Foreword

It is with great pleasure that I introduce you to this comprehensive guide, "Python for Absolute Beginners: The Ultimate Beginner's Guide to Learn Python Programming with Extensive Coverage on Data Science and Web Programming."

In today's digital age, Python stands out as a versatile and accessible language, making it an ideal choice for beginners eager to embark on their coding journey. What sets this book apart is its commitment to demystifying Python programming for absolute beginners, ensuring that the intricacies of coding are presented in an approachable and engaging manner.

The author's dedication to providing a solid foundation in Python is evident from the very first pages. From basic syntax to more advanced concepts, each chapter builds upon the last, creating a seamless learning experience. The inclusion of extensive coverage on data science and web programming reflects the practical applications of Python, making it a valuable resource for those aspiring to explore these dynamic fields.

One of the book's strengths lies in its clarity and simplicity. The author has successfully distilled complex programming concepts into digestible and easy-to-understand explanations, ensuring that even those with no prior coding experience can grasp the fundamentals with ease. The inclusion of real-world examples and hands-on exercises further enhances the learning process, allowing readers to apply their newfound knowledge in practical scenarios.

Whether you're a student looking to delve into the world of programming, a professional aiming to enhance your skill set, or simply an enthusiast eager to understand the language powering today's technological advancements, this book is your gateway to Python mastery. The step-by-step approach, coupled with a focus on data science and web programming, ensures that readers not only learn the fundamentals but also gain the skills necessary to tackle real-world projects.

As you embark on this exciting journey through "Python for Absolute Beginners," I encourage you to embrace the challenges and celebrate the victories. Remember that every line of code you write is a step closer to unlocking the vast possibilities that Python offers. May this book serve as a guiding light, illuminating the path to a rewarding and fulfilling journey in the world of Python programming.

Prof. Martin Anikwe
Director, International Linkages and Collaborations
Enugu State University of Science and Technology, Nigeria

Table of Contents

Dedication   iii
About the Author   iv
Acknowledgements   v
Preface   vi
Foreword   x
Table of contents   xi
Introduction   xiii

Chapter 1:
Python Syntax   **1**

Chapter 2:
Data types   **6**

Chapter 3:
Operators in python   **20**

Chapter 4:
Control flow statements   **40**

Chapter 5:
Looping statements   **45**

Chapter 6:
Strings   **53**

Chapter 7:
Lists   **72**

Chapter 8:
Tuples   **89**

Chapter 9:
Dictionaries   **97**

Chapter 10:
Sets   **110**

Chapter 11:
Functions   **119**

Chapter 12:
Modules 132

Chapter 13:
Files 140

Chapter 14:
OOP in Python 154

Chapter 15:
Exceptions 183

Chapter 16:
Testing 191

Chapter 17:
Asynchronous Programming with Asyncio 197

Chapter 18:
Requests in Python 206

Chapter 19:
Web scrapping in Python 216

Chapter 20:
Logging in python 228

Chapter 21:
Multithreading in python 235

Chapter 22:
Properties and descriptors 244

Chapter 23:
Exploring the Power of Data Science 262

Chapter 24:
Building web apps with Django 300

Index 327

Introduction

Imagine you work in marketing agency where your weekly responsibility involves sending email summaries to multiple clients, detailing their social media performance. These summaries encompass various metrics such as follower growth, engagement rates, and future strategies or plans.

Because you're manually composing and sending these emails, it is not only time-consuming but also stressful. There are occasions when certain clients are overlooked, or vital information is omitted from the summaries.

Despite your dedication and determination, you can't seem to overcome these recurring blunders.

It seems as if you're simply incompetent for the job.

Now, imagine that you have an experience in computer programming! You can leverage on your programming skills to automate the email sending process.

By writing a simple computer program, you can instruct the computer to perform these tasks for you.

But this requires the knowledge of a programming language and raises the question of which programming language to learn.

Sure, there are many programming languages available today, but Python stands out as a simple, elegant, powerful and multipurpose programming language that you can use for a wide range of programming tasks.

Python Programming

Python is a general-purpose programming language originally designed by Guido Van Rossum in the 1980s but released in 1991. It was named after his favourite show, Monty Python's Flying Circus.

It is an open-source programming language and is managed by Python Software Foundation (PSF). As an open-source programming language, you can access, modify, and distribute it, even for commercial purposes.

Python is an interpreted language, which means that you do not need to compile your programs before running them. Instead, the Python interpreter reads and executes your code, translating them into machine codes.

Also, Python is an object-oriented programming language, meaning you can organize your programs in classes and objects. This way, you can write programs that are not only reusable but easy to maintain and update.

Why Python?

Python is widely used in different fields of studies and industries for problem-solving and creating innovative software solutions. So many projects have been successfully implemented with Python in the areas of sciences, education, health care, hospitality and entertainment.

Surely, there are lots of other programming languages with outstanding features, but Python stands out in the following ways.

1. Simple and easy to learn

One of the significant objectives of Python as a language is readability and ease of expressing concepts in fewer lines of code. The syntax is concise, clear and easy to read.

Python is not only easy to read but to learn. This makes it an ideal programming language for beginners.

Also, experienced programmers in other languages can easily pick up the language and start writing programs with it almost immediately.

Surely, the simplicity of learning Python explains why it is being used to teach children the principles of programming.

2. Versatility

One of the reasons behind the popularity of Python is its versatility. It can be used for a wide range of projects including web development, data visualization and analysis, game development and much more.

Many top companies across the world are either using Python or implementing a part of their application using Python. Companies like Google, DropBox, Uber, Netflix, BitLy, Instagram and YouTube have used or are still using Python in their technology stacks.

Also, Python scripts can easily be integrated with applications written in other programming languages like Java, C/C++ and .NET languages, making it an excellent tool to glue together large software components.

3. Online Community

Python has a vast and supportive online community with lots of experienced developers willing to help as you journey into programming and beyond. There are also tons of educational resources available in form of online documentation, forums, mailing lists and conferences around the world.

These communities provide you with opportunities to connect with other programmers, facilitating the exchange of ideas and knowledge.

4. Efficiency

Productivity is of the essence to any programmer. Programs written with Python are considerably shorter than the equivalents in programming languages such as Java and C++.

Hence, you can write more programs in a lesser period compared to most other programming languages. In other words, it helps you do more with less time. This not only makes you more efficient but also more productive.

As an interpreted language, you get an immediate result whenever you make changes in the program. There is no need for compilation and recompilation that is obtainable in compiled languages.

This explains why Python is used for rapid application development (RAD) and as a tool for prototyping.

5. Extensive libraries

Python has vast libraries and third-party tools that can make things easier. Apart from the numerous standard libraries that come with Python, there are also myriads of powerful and tested third-party tools freely available at your disposal.

These are pre-written codes that solve a particular problem and with these libraries, you don't have to reinvent the wheel as you can easily integrate these libraries into your program.

Some of the popular libraries in Python include Panda for data analysis, matplotlib for visualization, Sci-kit learn for machine learning and much more.

Installing Python

Python is free and can be downloaded from its official website - python.org. There are different Python releases for different operating systems, so be sure to download the latest stable version for your operating system.

Once you've downloaded the Python installer for your operating system, you should run it to initiate the installation process. Follow the installation wizard carefully, paying attention to any prompts or options provided.

> ### Pro Tip
> *An important step, especially for Windows installation is to select the option that adds Python to your system's PATH. This step ensures that your operating system recognizes Python's location, making it easier to use from the command line or terminal.*

After completing the successful installation of Python on your computer, you gain access to an interactive environment where you can directly interact with Python and execute commands in real-time. This interactive environment is commonly referred to as a Python interpreter or shell.

You can initiate the interactive session by simply typing the word "python" or "Python3" in your terminal or console.

```
C:\Users>python
Python 3.12.1 (tags/v3.12.1:2305ca5, Dec  7 2023, 22:03:25) [MSC v.1937 64 bit (AMD64)] on win32
Type "help", "copyright", "credits" or "license" for more information.
>>> 
```

This will launch the Python interpreter, allowing you to interactively execute Python code.

The version of Python installed on your device will be displayed, followed by the appearance of the chevron symbol (>>>) or three arrows, indicating a line of input, where you can enter Python code and execute it interactively.

However, if it's not installed on your device, you will get an error message indicating "*command not found.*"

This interactive session is also known as REPL, which stands for **read, evaluate, print, and loop**. With REPL you can interact with the Python interpreter. You can directly type Python codes and have them run immediately.

```
C:\Users>python
Python 3.12.1 (tags/v3.12.1:2305ca5, Dec  7 2023, 22:03:25) [MSC v.1937 64 bit (AMD64)] on win32
Type "help", "copyright", "credits" or "license" for more information.
>>> 5 + 5
10
>>>
```

Lines that start with triple arrows are for inputs while lines without arrows are for outputs from the interpreter.

You can write some codes to perform some simple calculations and immediately after you hit the enter key, the interpreter will run the codes and display the result in the terminal.

To exit the interactive session, simply type CTRL Z.

```
C:\Users>python
Python 3.12.1 (tags/v3.12.1:2305ca5, Dec  7 2023, 22:03:25) [MSC v.1937 64 bit (AMD64)] on win32
Type "help", "copyright", "credits" or "license" for more information.
>>> 5 + 5
10
>>> ^Z

C:\Users>
```

Writing programs with the IDEs

IDE stands for Integrated Development Environment. It is a graphical user interface that allows programmers to write, edit, run and debug and debug programs in one place.

IDEs provide a convenient way to write programs and most of the code you will ever write will be done using this tool. Unlike the interactive session where code vanishes upon exiting, IDEs enable the preservation of your programs by saving them into files.

There are so many IDEs you can use for programming in Python including Sublime Text, PyCharm, Visual Studio Code and even the IDLE that is shipped with Python Interpreter.

However, Visual Studio Code stands out as one of the most popular and widely used IDEs by developers. It runs on Windows, Linux and macOS.

You can get this software from the <u>Visual Studio website</u> for free.

Simply, download and install it on your computer.

Once you have installed Visual Studio Code, create a new file by choosing the "File" ->"New File" option.

Type the following code in the text editor in the editor provided by the IDE and save the file with a .py extension to indicate that it is a Python script or file.

```
1  print('hello world')
```

Use the "Run" option to execute your Python code in the IDE.

Pro Tip
When you install Visual Studio Code (VSCode) for the first time, it comes with basic support for a variety of programming languages and features. However, to enhance the development experience specifically for Python, you need to install the Python extension.

To install the Python extension for Visual Studio Code, navigate to the Extensions view by clicking on the Extensions icon in the Activity Bar on the side. Look for the official "Python" extension developed by Microsoft and click the "Install" button. Once the installation is complete, you may need to reload VSCode to activate the extension. After reloading, you'll have access to a range of Python-specific features, including intelligent code completion, debugging support, linting, and more.

## Chapter I

PYTHON SYNTAX

"The most disastrous thing that you can ever learn is your first programming language."

- Alan Kay

Imagine that you are new to a foreign country with a different language and the only way to communicate with the locals is through their own language. Simply understanding the meanings of individual words is insufficient; you must also comprehend how to combine the words to construct coherent statements. However, if you pay good attention, you will see a pattern. You will discover that there are certain rules to be observed when trying to put the words together into statements. These rules are called syntax.

Learning outcome

In this chapter, you will learn:
- To write comments
- To use indentations and white spaces for code blocks and enhance readability
- To assign values to variables

Introduction

In every language, whether it is a natural language like English, French, or Spanish, or a programming language, there are rules that govern its structure. In natural languages, these rules are referred to as grammatical rules, while in programming languages, they are known as syntax.

The syntax is the rules that govern how you write programs in a programming language. Without adhering to these rules, it's impossible to make meaningful statements in any language.

Interestingly, the syntax for Python is simple and adhering to proper syntax is crucial in ensuring that the code is valid, readable, and can be executed without errors.

Some key aspects of Python syntax include:
- Comments
- Indentation

- Variables
- Data Types
- Control Flow
- Functions

Comments

Comments are used to document code and provide explanations. They are not executable and are ignored by the interpreter.

In Python, any piece of text that is preceded by a hash symbol (#) is considered a comment. To write a single-line comment in Python, simply type a hash symbol (#) followed by the comment text.

```
#writing a single line comment
#my first program
```

To write comments that spans across multiple lines, you can use triple quotes (""") to enclose the comment text. This type of comment is called a multiline comment.

```
"""
This is a multi-line comment
"""
```

Indentations and white spaces

In Python, indentations and white spaces are used to indicate the grouping and hierarchy of code blocks. Instead of relying on curly braces ({ }) or other symbols to delimit code blocks, Python employs indentation as the primary method for defining its code structure.

Indentation is typically done using four spaces or a tab character and is used to indicate the beginning and end of code blocks, such as loops, conditional statements, and function definitions.

```
#indentations and spaces
for num in [1,2,3,4,5]:
    #print num
```

```
print(num)
```

Here, the indentation is used to indicate statements under the for statement should be treated a single unit or a code block.

Variables

Variables are used to associate a name with a value. To declare a variable in Python, a name is provided followed by an assignment operator '=' and the value.

Take a look at this example:

```
num =   5
```

In the example, a variable named num is assigned to the value 5.

By assigning a value to a variable, you can refer to a given value through the name of the variable.

```
result = num + 4
print(result)
```

Output:

9

Here, the variable num is used to refer to the value of 5. Hence, 5 + 4 will give 9.

In some programming languages, it is common to define a variable and assign its value later in the program. However, Python requires variables to be assigned immediately upon declaration.

Also, unlike many other languages where variables are declared with a specific type, Python does not require variable declaration. Variables are dynamically typed, meaning they are assigned a value without explicitly stating their type.

> ### Pro Tip
> *A variable can be assigned an integer type and subsequently reassigned a string type. Upon assigning a new value to the variable, it replaces the previous value associated with it.*

Choosing a variable name

While you have the freedom to choose any name for your variables, it is essential to ensure that names accurately describe the associated value or object.

By using meaningful and descriptive variable names, you can make your code more understandable, allowing easier comprehension for yourself and others who may read or maintain your code in the future.

> **Pro Tip**
> *You should avoid using single letters or meaningless names as variables names of variables.*

Take a look at the following statements:

```
age = 25
a = 25
```

Using the variable name "age" instead of simply "a" would be a more suitable choice for enhancing code readability. By using "age" as the variable name, it provides clear and descriptive information about the value it represents, making the code easier to understand.

Overall, here are key things to keep in mind when choosing a variable name:
- Variable names can contain letters, numbers and underscore characters.
- Variable names are case-sensitive which means that the name adam is different from Adam.
- Variable names cannot begin with a number or contain special characters like @, $, %, *.
- Variable names cannot contain spaces.
- Reserved words or keywords cannot be used as variable names.

Summary

In this chapter, you learnt how to write comments. You learnt how to use proper indentations and white spaces. Additionally, you learnt how to assign values to variables and the rules for naming variables.

Practice Exercises

1. What are the reasons for the popularity of Python?
2. How is python interpreted?
3. What are the applications of Python?
4. Mention 5 companies using python in their tech stack.
5. How do you write comments in python?
6. Write a Python program that displays "Hello world"

## Chapter 2

DATA TYPES

"It's difficult to imagine the power that you're going to have when so many different sorts of data are available."
- Tim Berners-Lee

Data is actually a huge part of our everyday life. Whether we're shopping for groceries, having a chat with our friends, or just mindlessly scrolling through our social media feeds, we're constantly using or creating data. If you take a moment and reflect on this, you will be amazed to discover how involved data is in everything we do. Given the abundance of data around us, it becomes essential to organize and categorize them in order to make meanings from them. In the realm of computers, data is classified into different types, also known as data types.

Learning outcome

In this chapter, you will learn:
- Basic data types like numeric, strings, booleans and sequences.
- Various numeric data types including integers, floats and complex numbers.
- Sequences or collections such as lists, tuples, dictionaries and much more.
- How to use the print() and input() built-in functions.

Introduction

Consider the number 2 and the word 'hello.' While both qualify as data, however, they differ in terms of the operations applicable to them. You can perform mathematical additions on numbers, but you cannot do the same to a piece of text.

Python provides support for a diverse range of data types, encompassing numbers, strings, lists, tuples, dictionaries, and more. This versatility in Python empowers programmers to efficiently and effectively handle various types of data.

The following categorization presents various data types in Python:

- Numeric
- Strings
- Booleans
- Sequences

Numeric

Numeric data types consist of integers, floats, and complex numbers. Integers represent whole numbers without any decimal places. Floats, on the other hand, are numbers that include decimal places. Complex numbers are a combination of real and imaginary parts, allowing for operations involving both components.

Here are examples of numeric data types in Python:

Integers	1,2,5,10, -100
Floats	1.05, -99.5, 0.005
Complex	2 - 1j, 4 - 6j

Integers

Integers are simply whole numbers. They can be positive or negative but without fractional or decimal parts. Numbers like 1, 777, -101 and even 0 are Integers.

However, integers are not only numbers in base 10, but also include whole numbers in other number systems like - binary, octal or hexadecimal.

> **Pro Tip**
> *Number systems are ways of representing numbers. Naturally, we count in the decimal number system. Here, the smallest digit is 0 and the largest is 9. In computing, numbers are represented internally in computers in binaries. At the basic or machine level, computers only understand instructions in the form of zeros and ones. Programming languages such as Python allow programmers to write codes in letters, numbers and symbols, but these instructions are converted to streams of 0s and 1s.*
> *There are essentially four kinds of number systems used in computing and programming in particular and they include:*
>
> - *Decimal*
> - *Binary*
> - *Hexadecimal*
> - *Octal*

Now, let's briefly explain the important number systems that you may likely encounter while working with integers in python.

Binary Numbers

A binary number is a number expressed in base 2 or binary number system. Binary numbers have two digits - 0 and 1.

Octal Numbers

Octal numbers are numbers expressed in base 8 or octal number system. In this number system, the digits range from 0 to 7.

Decimal Numbers

These are numbers expressed in base 10. Numbers in base 10 consist of 10 digits with 0 being the smallest and 9 being the largest.

Hexadecimal Numbers

Hexadecimal numbers are numbers in base 16. They have 16 digits with 0 being the smallest and F being the largest. The digit F is equivalent to 15 in the decimal number system.

The table below presents the digits available in the binary, octal, decimal and hexadecimal number systems.

Binary	Octal	Decimal	Hexadecimal
0	0	0	0
1	1	1	1
	2	2	2
	3	3	3
	4	4	4
	5	5	5
	6	6	6
	7	7	7
		8	8
		9	9
			A

			B
			C
			D
			E
			F

Floats

Floats or floating point numbers are numbers that contain decimal points. They can be positive or negative. The following numbers are examples of floating-point numbers:

- 0.004
- -1.50
- 23.00045

Complex Numbers

Similar to mathematical concepts, complex numbers consist of a real and an imaginary part. For example, 2 + 5j is a complex number with 2 being the real part and 5 being the imaginary part.

With python, you can easily extract the real and imaginary parts using the real and imag attributes of the number as shown below:

```
number = 2 + 5j
print(number.real)
print(number.imag)
```

Outputs:
2.0
5.0

Number Type Conversion

Number type conversion is a fundamental aspect of Python programming. The need for type conversion often arises when you want to perform operations or comparisons between different numeric types.

To achieve this, Python provides specific functions that enable you to convert numbers or even strings into a preferred numeric type. These functions are:

- **int():** Converts a value to an integer.
- **float():** Converts a value to a floating-point number.
- **complex():** Converts a value to a complex number.

```
num = 20
int_num = int(num)
print(int_num)
float_num = float(num)
print(float_num)
complex_num = complex(num)
print(complex_num)
```

Outputs:
20
20.0
(20+0j)

Binary, Octal and Hexadecimal Conversions

You have the flexibility to convert between binary, decimal, octal, and hexadecimal representations using the bin(), oct(), hex(), and int() functions.

```
num = 9
#Binary
print(bin(num))
#Octal
print(oct(num))
#Decimal
print(int(num))
#Hexadecimal
print(hex(num))
```

Outputs:
0b1001
0o11
9
0x9

Mathematical functions

These are functions that are used to perform mathematically related operations on numbers. Some of these functions include:

- abs()
- pow()
- round()
- math.trunc()
- math.floor()
- math.ceil()

abs()

This function returns the absolute value of a given number. It strips of the the unary signs in a number.

> **Pro Tip:**
> *Unary signs refer to the use of positive (+) or negative (-) symbols to denote the sign of a number in a unary numeral system.*

```python
print(abs(-10))
print(abs(1.05))
print(abs(+0.5))
```

Outputs:
10
1.05
0.5

pow()

This function returns the value corresponding to the number raised to a given power. It accepts two arguments, the first being the number that you want to exponentiate, and the second being the power.

```
print(pow(2,2))
print(pow(2,3))
print(pow(2,4))
```

Outputs:
4
8
16

round()

This function rounds or approximates a number to the nearest whole number. In other words, it takes a decimal or fractional value and adjusts it to the closest integer value. If the decimal part is 0.5 or greater, the number is rounded up; if it's less than 0.5, the number is rounded down.

```
print(round(10.2))
print(round(10.5))
print(round(10.6))
print(round(10.9))
```

Outputs:
10
10
11
11

math.trunc()

This is used to truncate a floating-point number towards zero, effectively removing the decimal part of the number and returning the integer part.

However, to use this function, you have to import the math module.

```
import math

print(math.trunc(10.2))
print(math.trunc(10.9))
```

Outputs:
10
10

math.floor()

The function operates similarly to the trunc() function. It removes the decimal part of a floating-point number, effectively truncating the value and returning a whole number.

Unlike rounding, which may round up or down based on the fractional part, this function simply discards the decimal component, resulting in the integer part of the original floating-point number without any rounding.

```
import math

print(math.floor(10.2))
print(math.floor(10.9))
```

Outputs:
10
10

math.ceil()

This function approximates a floating-point number to a whole number, greater than the integer part of the number.

```
import math

print(math.ceil(10.2))
print(math.ceil(10.9))
```

Outputs:
11
11

Formatting numbers

The format() method allows you to control how numbers, strings, or other data types are formatted for display. It's particularly helpful when you want to display numbers in a specific way, such as controlling the number of decimal places, adding commas as thousand separators, displaying numbers in scientific notation, or specifying padding for alignment in strings.

Take a look at this example:

```
#rounding to 2 decimal places
result = '{:.2f}'.format(1.35)
print(result)

#rounding to 1 decimal place
result = '{:.1f}'.format(1.35)
print(result)

#including per cent to a number
result = '{}%'.format(1.35)
print(result)
```

Outputs:
1.35
1.4
1.35%

Random Numbers

The random module provides a collection of functions for generating random numbers and conducting various randomization tasks.

Whether you're developing simulations, games, statistical models, or cryptographic applications, the random module serves as your essential tool for infusing an element of unpredictability.

Here are some of the popular methods in the random module.

randint()

This method is used to generate random integer numbers. To use this method, you need to provide arguments that specify the range within which the random integers should be generated.

```
from random import randint
num = randint(1,5)
print(num)
```

random()

This method generates floating point numbers within the range of 0.0 (inclusive) and 1.0 (exclusive).

```
from random import random
num = random()
print(num)
```

choice()

This method is used to randomly select and return a single item from a given sequence. To use this method, you need to provide a sequence such as lists, tuples, or string as an argument, and the method then randomly picks one element from that sequence.

```
from random import choice
L = ['apple', 'grape', 'mango', 'banana']
result = choice(L)
print(result)
```

randrange()

This method behaves like the randint(), except that it allows you to specify not only the range of values but also an optional step value, enabling you to skip values within that range. The syntax is as follows:

randrange(start, stop, step)

```
from random import randrange

result = randrange(1,10,2)
print(result)
```

Strings

Strings are used to represent textual data. They are enclosed within quotation marks, which can be either single ('), double ("), or triple (''' or """). They can contain a combination of letters, numbers, and symbols, allowing for versatile representation of textual information.

The following are examples of strings:

```
colour = 'orange'
desc = "There are 3 oranges in the box."
number = '1234'
contact = '55 Hillview Avenue, Trans Ekulu'
```

> **Pro Tip:**
> *Strings are used to store various types of information, such as names of individuals, addresses, or descriptions of objects or concepts.*

Booleans

The Boolean data type is characterized by two distinct values: True and False. It is specifically utilized to represent logical values, where True denotes a condition that is considered true or valid, and False indicates a condition that is false or invalid.

```
val1 = True
val2 = False
```

It is important to note that in Python, the values True and False for boolean data type are written with capital letters (T and F) at the beginning, while the remaining letters are in lowercase.

Sequences

Sequences often referred to as collections, allows you to organize and store multiple elements in a specific order. These data types include:

- Lists
- Tuples
- Dictionaries
- Sets
- Strings
- Files

In addition to these basic data types, Python also supports more advanced data types, such as arrays, classes, and objects.

print() function

The print function is a built-in function that allows you to display output on the console or terminal. It is commonly used to print text or the values of variables and expressions during program execution.

The print function accepts one or more arguments, which can be strings, numbers, variables, or expressions, and displays them as output on the console.

```
print("hello")
print([1,2,3,4,5])
```

Output:
hello
[1, 2, 3, 4, 5]

The print function by default results in a new line.

Take a look at this example:

```
print("apple")
print("orange")
print("mango")
```

Output:
apple
orange
Mango

However, if you do not to wish to have a newline anytime you used the print() function, you can change it through the end argument.

For example:

```
print("apple", end="")
print("orange", end="")
print("mango", end="")
```

Output:
apple orange mango

Also, the print() function has the flexibility to accept a variable number of arguments, which are then displayed as a string with white space separating them.

```
#print() function with multiple arguments
print("greet", "me", "!")
```

Output:
greet me !

Input() function

The input() function in Python is used to obtain input from users. It displays a prompt to the user, requesting them to provide text or data. The user can then input their response, and upon pressing the enter key, it signifies that they have finished supplying the input .

For example:

```
name = input()
print("your name is", name)
```

Also, the input() function takes an optional argument in form of a string, as a way of informing the user of the required information to supply.

```
name = input("What is your name: ")
print("your name is", name)
```

Summary

You learnt various data types in Python including the numeric types, strings and boolean data type and sequences. You also learnt their characteristics, how to use them, and the operations you can perform on them. You used the print() function to display output to console and the input() function to receive input from the user.

Practice Exercises

1. What do you understand by data type in Python?
2. List common data types in Python.
3. Mention the different numeric data types.
4. What is a number system?
5. Write a program that prompts the user to provide their name.

## Chapter 3

OPERATIONS IN PYTHON

"The idea behind digital computers may be explained by saying that these machines are intended to carry out any operation which could be done by a human computer."

- Alan Turing

As humans, we have this innate need to measure things. We're constantly seeking to quantify and understand the world around us. Whether it's measuring time, distance, or even emotions, we have this inherent desire to put things into measurable terms. We measure success, happiness, and even personal growth. It's as if measuring things gives us a sense of progress and helps us set goals for ourselves. It's fascinating how deeply ingrained this instinct is within us. Interestingly, in the realm of programming, we can apply a similar concept using a set of tools known as operators. These operators allow us to perform calculations and comparisons, providing a means to measure and manipulate data within the digital world.

Learning outcome

In this chapter, you will learn:
- To use various operator types.
- To create simple and compound expressions.
- To use operator precedence to determine how compound expressions are evaluated.

Introduction

An operator is a symbol or word(s) that denotes the kind of operation to be performed on values.

Take a look at the following line of code.

```
1 + 2
```

The plus (+) symbol is used to indicate addition.

When the interpreter encounters the plus symbol (+) between numbers, it interprets it as an expression and executes the addition operation on the given values.

So, an expression is formed by combining values and operators. By combining operators, such as the plus symbol (+), with values, you construct an expression capable of being assessed to yield a singular value.

For example, 5 - 3 is an expression with the minus operator (-) and values (5 and 3). In this case, the operator - denotes subtraction, and the outcome is 2.

When multiple expressions are present, Python continuously evaluates each individual expression until they are reduced to a single value.

For instance:

In the expression, 2 + 3 + 4, the value 2 is added to 3, which evaluates to 5, and then 4 is added to 5, which gives 9.

A lot of times, you would be assigning a name to an expression. By doing so, you can conveniently refer to the expression using its assigned name whenever needed.

For example:

```
sum = 2 + 3
```

So, if you ever need to refer to this expression later on, you can simply use the name "sum."

Types of operators

There are basically six types of operators in python and they include:

- Arithmetic
- Relational
- Logical
- Bitwise
- Identity
- Membership

Arithmetic operators

These operators are used to perform arithmetic operations or calculations. Here are the commonly used arithmetic operators in Python.

- Addition (+)
- Subtraction (-)
- Multiplication (*)
- Division (/)
- Floor division (//)
- Modulus (%)
- Exponentiation (**)

The addition operator (+) is used for adding numbers, while the subtraction operator (−) is used in performing subtractions. The multiplication operator (*) is used for multiplications in numbers.

The single forward slash (/) is for division and when you use a single forward slash (/) as the division operator, the result is always a floating-point number. This type of division is known as true division.

The double forward slash (//) is also used for a kind of division called the floor or integer division. The outcome of this division is an integer value. When numbers are divided using the integer division operator, the decimal points are removed retaining only the integer number.

The double asterisk (**) is used as an operator for exponentiation, and the percentage sign (%) is used as an operator for modulus.

Modulus is the same thing as the remainder.

For instance, 5 divided by 2 will give 2 and a remainder of 1.

2 is the quotient while 1 is the remainder or modulus.

Below is an example program that demonstrates the usage of arithmetic operators in calculations:

```
#arithmetic operations

# Addition
num1 = 2
num2 = 3
sum = num1 + num2
print("Addition: ", sum)
```

```python
# Subtraction
num3 = 12
num4 = 8
diff = num3  - num4
print("Subtraction: ", diff)

# Multiplication
num5 = 4
num6 = 6
product = num5 * num6
print("Multiplication: ", product)

# Division
num7 = 20
num8 = 3
quotient = num7 / num8
print("True Division: ", quotient)

# Floor Division
num9 = 20
num10 = 3
result = num9 // num10
print("True Division: ", result)

# Modulo
num11 = 17
num12 = 4
remainder = num11 % num12
print("Modulo:", remainder)

# Exponentiation
base = 2
power = 5
result = base ** power
print("Exponentiation:", result)

# Floor Division
num13 = 15
num14 = 7
floor_division = num13 // num14
```

```
print("Floor Division:", floor_division)
```

Output:

Addition: 5
Subtraction: 4
Multiplication: 24
True Division: 6.666666666666667
True Division: 6
Modulo: 1
Exponentiation: 32
Floor Division: 2

Binary and unary operators

Most arithmetic operators are binary operators, meaning that they work on two values or operands.

An expression like 2 * 3 has the multiplication operator * and two operands 2 and 3. 2 is the left operand, while 3 is the right operand.

However, some arithmetic operators are unary operators and work on a single operator. For instance, negative and positive signs like + and − are unary operators representing mathematical signs.

+   Unary plus
−   Unary minus

For example:

-5
+10

Representing mathematical expressions in Python

Arithmetic operators allow you to translate mathematical expressions into Python expressions.

Let's convert a few mathematical expressions into their corresponding Python expressions:

Mathematical expression: $y = 2x - 1$
Python expression: y = 2*x - 1

Mathematical expression:	$z = x3 + y2 + 5$
Python expression:	$x**3 + y**2 + 5$

Grouping expressions with parenthesis

Parentheses are used to group expressions together. Through the use of parentheses, you can break down complex expressions into smaller, more manageable chunks, thereby ensuring the accurate calculation of each sub-expression.

Take a look at the example below:

```
# using parentheses for grouping expressions
# without parentheses
result1 = 2 + 3 * 4
print("Result without parentheses:", result)

# with parentheses
result2 = (2 + 3) * 4
print("Result with parentheses:", result2)
```

Output:
14
20

In the first expression, without parentheses, Python adheres to the order of operations (PEMDAS), executing multiplication before addition, yielding 2 + 12 = 14.

However, in the second expression, the parentheses alters the order of operations, emphasizing the calculation of the grouped addition before other operations, resulting in (2 + 3) * 4 = 5 * 4 = 20.

> **Pro Tip:**
> *The use of parentheses alters the grouping and precedence of operations within an expression. Ensure that you group the right expressions together. If not, you may get the wrong result.*

Rules of Operator Precedence

Expressions in Python are executed according to the operator's order of precedence. It's important to note that expressions are not evaluated strictly from left to right or right to left. Instead, the order of precedence determines which operators are evaluated first in an expression.

Python evaluates expressions based on the precedence of the operators using a set of rules. These rules are similar to the rules for algebraic expressions and are abbreviated as PEDMMAS.

Operators are evaluated in the following order.

1. Parenthesis
2. Exponentiation
3. Division
4. Multiplication
5. Modulus
6. Addition
7. Subtraction

Operators that are contained in a pair of parenthesis are evaluated before those that are outside of the parenthesis. This is followed by exponentiation, division, multiplication, modulus, addition and then subtraction.

Now, let's see how it works through the example below:

```
#arithmetic operator precedence
result = 2 + 2 - 2 * 2 / 2 ** 2 % 2
print(result)
#using parenthesis to confirm precedence
result = 2 + 2 - ((2 * (2 / (2 ** 2))) % 2)
print(result)
```

Output:
3.0
3.0

From the example above, you can see the expressions are evaluated according to the precedence of operators.

Relational Operators

Relational operators, also known as comparison operators, are utilized to compare two or more values for equality.

Particularly, they are used to establish if two values are equal, less or greater than each other and are mostly used in control statements for decision-making.

The following are relational operators and their meaning.

- Greater than >
- Less than <
- Greater or equal to >=
- Less or equal to <=
- Equality ==
- Not Equality !=

The greater than (>) returns True if the operand on the left is larger than the operator on the right.
The less than (<) returns True if the operand on the left is smaller than the operator on the right.
Greater or equal to (>=) returns True if the operand on the left is equivalent or larger than the operator on the right.
Less or equal to (<=) returns True if the operand on the left is equivalent or smaller than the operator on the right.
The equality operator (==) returns True if the left and right operators are equivalent, while the not equality operator (!=) returns True if the operands are not equivalent.

> **Pro Tip:**
> *Keep in mind that the equality operator (==) is not the same as equal to (=). The equality operator (==) is a relational operator used in comparing values, while the equal sign (=) is an assignment operator used in assigning values to a variable.*

Truthy and falsey values

A value that is considered "truthy" is one that is evaluated as equivalent to True in a Boolean context. On the other hand, a value that is considered "falsey" is one that is evaluated as equivalent to False in a Boolean context.

For example, any number greater than 0, a non-empty list, or a non-empty string is evaluated as True and is considered truthy. Conversely, the number 0, an empty string, or an empty list is evaluated as False and is considered falsey.

In the following example, relational operators are utilized to compare values.

```python
#relational operations

# Greater than
value1 = 7
value2 = 4
result1 = value1 > value2
print("Greater than:", result1)

# Less than
value3 = 8
value4 = 5
result2 = value3 < value4
print("Less than:", result2)

# Greater than or equal to
value5 = 5
value6 = 5
result3 = value5 >= value6
print("Greater than or equal to:", result3)

# Less than or equal to
value7 = 9
value8 = 9
result4 = value7 <= value8
print("Less than or equal to:", result4)

#equality
value9 = 4
value10 = 7
result5 = value9 == value10
print("Equal to:", result5)

#not equality
value11 = 3
value12 = 2
result6 = value11 == value12
print("Equal to:", result6)
```

Output:
Greater than: True

Less than: False
Greater than or equal to: True
Less than or equal to: True
Equal to: False
Equal to: False

Logical operators

Logical operators allow you to join together boolean values or expressions to create a more complex expression. This compound expression is then examined to determine if it ultimately resolves to either True or False. The following are examples of logical operators:

- and
- or
- not

and Operator

The "and" operator is used to combine two or more expressions into a single complex expression. When the "and" operator is used to combine expressions, each individual expression must evaluate to True for the overall outcome to be True. If any of the expressions evaluates to False, the entire expression will evaluate to False.

or operator

The "or" operator is also used to combine two or more expressions. Unlike the and operator, the combined expression evaluates to True, if any of the individual expressions evaluate to True. It evaluates to False if all the expressions evaluate to False.

not operator

The "not" operator negates the boolean value of the operand, returning True if the operand is False, and False if the operand is True.

Overall, these logical operators allow you to build complex conditions and make decisions based on multiple criteria.

In the following example, the logical operators are used to combine expressions and values together.

```python
# Logical operations
value1 = 4
value2 = 8

# Logical AND operator
result1 = (value1 > 0) and (value2 < 15)
print(result1)

# Logical OR operator
result2 = (value1 == 0) or (value2 > 20)
print(result2)

# Logical NOT operator
result3 = not (value1 > value2)
print(result3)
```

Output:
True
False
True

Bitwise operators

Any operation that involves the use or manipulation of data in its binary form is considered a bitwise operation.

Bitwise operations are done using the bitwise operators. With these operators, you can perform all sorts of data manipulation on data at the basic or binary level.

Bitwise operations are highly efficient and renowned for their exceptional speed due to their binary-level execution and are often used in operations where speed and efficiency are of uttermost importance.

Hence, bitwise operations are widely used in encryptions, communications over networks, graphics and much more.

The following are examples of bitwise operators:

- Bitwise and &
- Bitwise or |

- Bitwise xor $\wedge$
- Bitwise leftshift $<<$
- Bitwise right shift $>>$
- Bitiwse not $\sim$

Bitwise AND operator

This operator is represented with the symbol &. It returns 1 if both operands have a binary digit of 1 in the same position, and 0 if otherwise.

You can also determine the outcome of the bitwise and operation at any given position using the formula:

(A & B)i = Ai x Bi

This is demonstrated in the figure below, where the respective bits in a given position are multiplied.

```
                              1 1 0 1
1 1 0 1 & 1 0 0 1   =      x  1 0 0 1
        bitwise and          1 0 0 1
```

> **Pro Tip:**
> *Converting an integer to its binary representation (bits) can be done using the bin() function. The bin() function returns a string representing the binary form of an integer.*

For better understanding, the following code expressed numbers in binary forms and outcomes are converted to binary.

```python
#bitwise and

num1 = 0b1101
num2 = 0b1011

result1 = bin(num1 & num2)
print(result1)
```

```
num3 = 0b100
num4 = 0b101

result2 = bin(num3 & num4)
print(result2)
```

Output:
0b1001
0b100

Bitwise OR operator

This operator returns 1 if one or both operands have a binary digit of 1 in any given position. If both operands have 0 at any given position, the outcome is 0. The bitwise or operator is represented with the symbol |.

Also, you can determine the outcome of bitwise or operation using the formula below.

(A | B)i = Ai + Bi

In the illustration above, 1 is returned if the sum of the binary digits in a given position is 1 or greater than 1. Now, let's further demonstrate it using the code below.

```
#bitwise or

num5 = 0b1101
num6 = 0b1001

result3 = bin(num5 | num6)
print(result3)

num7 = 0b100
```

```
num8 = 0b101

result4 = bin(num7 | num8)
print(result4)
```

Output:
0b1101
0b101

Bitwise XOR operator

The bitwise xor operator returns 1 if the bits in the same position are of opposing values. This means that, if the corresponding bits in a given position are both 1 or both 0, the outcome is 0.

The bitwise operator xor is represented with the symbol ^.

You can determine the outcome of the bitwise xor operation using the formula below.

(A | B)i = (Ai + Bi) mod 2

In the illustration below, the bits in a given position are first added. Then, the resulting value is divided by 2 and the remainder or modulus becomes the outcome.

1 1 0 1 ^ 1 0 0 1 = + 1 1 0 1 / 1 0 0 1 / (2)(1)(0)(2) %2 / 0 1 0 0

bitwise xor

The following example demonstrates the usage of the bitwise xor operator:

```
#bitwise xor

num9 = 0b1101
num10 = 0b1011

result5 = bin(num9 ^ num10)
print(result5)
```

```
num11 = 0b110111
num12 = 0b101011

result6 = bin(num11 ^ num12)
print(result6)
```

Output:
0b110
0b11100

Bitwise NOT Operator

The bitwise not operator is represented with the symbol ~. Unlike most bitwise operators that work on two sets of operands, the bitwise not operator is a unary operator that operates on a single operand.

It is used to perform logical negation and the outcome is determined with the formula below:

~Ai = 1 – Ai

This is illustrated in the figure below:

The bitwise not operator is illustrated in the code snippet below:

```
#bitwise not

num13 = 0b10
result7 = bin(~num13)
print(result7)
```

Output:

-0b11

Bitwise left shift operator

The bitwise left shift operator moves the bits of the first operand to the left by the number of positions specified by the second operand. The left-shifted bits are filled with zeros on the right side.

The bitwise left shift operator is represented with the symbol <<.

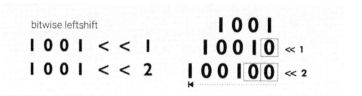

Here, is an example:

```
#bitwise leftshift

num14 = 0b1001

result8 = bin(num14 << 1)
print(result8)

result9 = bin(num14 << 2)
print(result9)

result10 = bin(num14 << 3)
print(result10)
```

Output:
0b10010
0b100100
0b1001000

Also, the bitwise left shift operator can be evaluated using the following formula.

A << n = Ax2n

So, 5 << 2 is the same thing as:
5×22 = 5×4 = 20

Bitwise right shift operator

The bitwise right shift operator in Python shifts the bits of the first operand to the right by the number of positions specified by the second operand. The right-shifted bits are padded with zeros on the left side. This operator is represented by the symbol ">>".

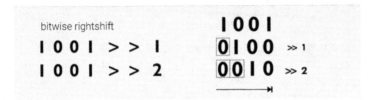

The code below demonstrates the bitwise right shift operations.

```
#bitwise right shift

num15 = 0b1001

result11 = bin(num15 >> 1)
print(result11)

result12 = bin(num15 >> 2)
print(result12)

result13 = bin(num15 >> 3)
print(result13)

result14 = bin(num15 >> 4)
print(result14)
```

Output:
0b100
0b10
0b1
0b0

Membership Operators

Membership operators are used to test whether a specific item or value is present in a sequence or collection. They are used to determine whether a given item or value is present in a sequence such as the list, tuple, sets and so on.

There are two membership operators in python and they include:

- In operator
- Not in operator

The "in" operator verifies the presence of a value within a sequence, such as a string, list, tuple, or set. On the other hand, the "not in" operator confirms the absence of a value within the sequence. If the value is not found, it returns True; otherwise, it returns False.

In the following example, the membership operators are utilized to ascertain the existence of specific values within a sequence.

```
# membership operators
nums = [1, 2, 3, 4, 5]
print(3 in nums)
greeting = "Hello there!"
print("there" in greeting)
print("world" in greeting)
```

Output:
True
True
False

Identity operators

Identity operators are used to compare the identity of two objects, checking if they refer to the same memory location. They are used to establish whether a given value is the same as another value.

Identity operators in Python go beyond just checking equality. They allow you to determine if two values are not only equivalent but also refer to the exact same object in memory.

In other words, even if two values may look alike and have the same content, they may not be the exact same object. So, identity comparison provides a way to distinguish between objects that are truly identical and those that are only equivalent.

There are two identity operators in python and they include:

- Is operator
- Is not operator

The "is" operator checks if two variables refer to the same object in memory. It returns True if the variables have the same identity, and False otherwise.

The "is not" operator checks if two variables do not refer to the same object in memory. It returns True if the variables have different identities, and False if they refer to the same object.

The code below provides an example of the use of identity operators in Python.

```
# identity operators

num1 = 5
num2 = 4
num3 = num1

print(num1 is num2)
print(num1 is num3)
print(num2 is num3)

num4 = 5
num5 = 10
print(num4 is not num5)
```

Output:
False
True
False
True

Summary

In this chapter, you learnt the different types of operators in Python. You used the arithmetic operators to perform addition, subtraction, multiplication, division, and other mathematical operations on numeric values. Also, you used the comparison operators to check for equality, inequality, greater than, less than, and other comparison conditions. You used the logical operators to combine boolean values and evaluate complex logical conditions. Additionally, you learnt how to structure expressions logically and how the operator precedence is used in evaluations of compound expressions.

Practice Exercises

1. What are the different types of operators in Python?
2. What is the meaning of operator precedence?
3. State the difference between expression and statement?
4. State 5 examples of arithmetic operators.
5. What is the use of parenthesis in operator precedence?
6. Write a program that calculates the area and volume of a rectangle and a cubiod.
7. Write a program that converts temperature in Celsius to Farenheit?
8. What is the advantages of bitwise operations.

## Chapter 4

CONTROL FLOW STATEMENTS

"When you change the way you look at things, the things you look at change."

- Max Planck

A typical computer program is executed in a linear manner, from top to bottom. This means that the first line of code gets executed before any other lines, and the last line is the final one to be executed. But what if we want to change the order of execution or repeat a specific piece of code multiple times? That's when control statements come into play. They allow us to control the flow of program execution and make our programs more dynamic. By incorporating control statements into our programs, we can create more dynamic and versatile software that responds to different conditions and user inputs.

Learning outcome

In this chapter, you will learn:
- Various types of control statements.
- To use if, elif, and else statements for decision making.
- To use nested if statements.

Introduction

Control flow statements in Python are programming constructs that allow you to alter the flow of execution in a program based on specific conditions. Typically, programs execute in a sequential manner, going from top to bottom and left to right.

However, there are situations where you may want to break away from this linear execution. That's when control flow statements come into play. By using control statements; you can create programs that make intelligent decisions.

There are three types of control statements in Python and they include:

1. Conditional statements
2. Looping statements
3. Jump statements

Conditional statements

Conditional statements allow you to execute specific blocks of code based on certain conditions. With conditional statements, you can break away from the linear execution of your program. This means that certain sections of code may or may not be executed, depending on the conditions you specify.

Conditional statements are incredibly powerful as they enable your program to adapt and respond intelligently to different scenarios. They make it possible to create dynamic and interactive programs that can react differently based on the input or current state of the program.

The main conditional statements in Python are:

- if statement
- if-else statement
- if-elif-else

If statements

The "if" statement is widely used and considered the most commonly employed conditional statement. It allows you to evaluate a condition and execute a specific block of code if the condition is true.

This is the syntax:

if condition:
    # Code to be executed if the condition is true

The "if" keyword marks the beginning of the statement, followed by the condition, which is an expression that determines whether the block of code will be executed or not. The colon (:) denotes the end of the condition and indicates that the following indented code block is associated with the "if" statement.

Take a look at this example:

```
#if statement
num = 4
if num % 2 == 0:
    print('an even number')
```

Output:
an even number

In the above example, the condition num % 2 == 0 needs to evaluate to True. If the remainder of num divided by 2 is equal to 0, it means that num is an even number, and the code block inside the "if" statement will be executed, resulting in the message "an even number" being printed.

Now, here is the problem.

The print() statement never executes if num is an odd number. To fix this, you can use an else statement. This way, you can specify what to do when the number is odd.

Else statement

The else statement in Python is used to provide a fallback block of code to be executed when none of the preceding condition(s) in an if statement are true.

In the previous example, there was no fallback option to handle the case when num is an odd number.

To address this, you can use an else statement to provide an alternative set of instructions that will be executed when the condition within the if statement is false.

For example:

```
#else statements
if num % 2 == 0:
    print('an even number')
else:
    print('an odd number)
```

Elif statements

The "elif" statement is used to introduce an alternative condition in an "if" statement. It allows you to check for additional conditions after the initial if statement and execute a different block of code if the preceding condition(s) are false, but the elif condition is true.

Here's an example to illustrate the usage:

```
#elif statement
if num % 2 == 0:
    print('an even number')
elif num % 2 != 0:
    print('an odd number')
```

In the above example, the if statement checks if num is an even number using the condition num % 2 == 0. If this condition is true, the code inside the if block is executed, printing the message 'an even number.'

The elif statement (short for "else if") introduces a new condition to be checked only if the preceding if condition is false. In this case, it checks whether num is not an even number using the condition num % 2 != 0. If this condition is true, the code inside the elif block is executed, printing the message 'an odd number.'

Now, let's create additional branches using multiple elif statements:

```
#multiple elif statement
if num % 2 == 0:
    print('an even number')
elif num % 3 == 0:
    print('divisible by 3')
elif num % 4 != 0:
    print('divisible by 4')
```

The program checks if the number is divisible by 2. If true, it prints "an even number".If the number is not divisible by 2, it checks if it is divisible by 3. If true, it prints "divisible by 3".If the number is not divisible by 2 or 3, it checks if it is not divisible by 4. If true, it prints "divisible by 4".

Nested if statements

Nested if statement is an if statement that is placed inside another if statement. They are particularly useful when you need to introduce more levels of conditions or perform more specific checks based on multiple conditions.

Take a look at this example:

```
#nested if statements
if num > 0:
    if num % 2 == 0:
        print('even number')
```

In this case, the program checks if num is greater than 0, and if so, it proceeds to check if num is even. The code block inside the inner if statement will only execute if both conditions are true.

> **Pro Tip:**
> *It's important to note that indentation is crucial in Python as it determines the block of code associated with each if statement. The inner if statement is indented further to indicate that it belongs to the outer if block.*

Summary

You learnt the various types of control statements and how they can be used to control the flow of execution in your program based on certain conditions or criteria. The if statement is used to execute a block of code if a certain condition is true. If the condition is false, the code block is skipped. The elif statement is used to check additional conditions after the initial if statement. The else statement is to used to provide a default block of code to be executed when none of the preceding conditions in an if-elif structure are true.

Practice Exercises

1. What does it mean to control the flow of programs?
2. Mention the three types of control statements.
3. Write a program that determines if a number is even or odd or prime.
4. Write a program to check whether a number is divisible by 3
5. Write a program that tests whether an input is an integer.
6. Write a program to determine if a person is eligible to vote or not (voting age is 18 years and above).
7. Write a program that accepts scores from user and displays the corresponding grade using the following criteria. F(0-39), E(40-44), D(45-49), C(50-59), B(60-69) and A(70 and above).

## Chapter 5

LOOPING STATEMENTS

"If at first you don't succeed, try, try again. Then quit. There's no point in being a damn fool about it."

- W. C. Fields

Imagine people moving in a circle. They keep going around and around until a specific condition is met or a certain number of repetitions are completed. This continuous circular movement can represent a loop in programming. In programming, we often use loops to perform repetitive tasks or iterate over a set of data. It's like going around the circle multiple times, executing the same set of instructions until a certain condition is satisfied. Just as the circular movement allows us to visit the same points again and again, loops enable us to revisit and reprocess a block of code until a desired outcome is achieved.

Learning outcome

In this chapter, you will learn:
- To use the for loop and while loop to execute codes repeatedly.
- To use the continue and break statements to break out of a loop.
- How to iterate over sequences using loops.

Introduction

Looping statements are used to execute a block of code repeatedly, allowing you to automate repetitive tasks and iterate over sequences or collections of data.

Python provides two main types of looping statements and they include:

1. For loop
2. While loop

For loop

A for loop is used to iterate over a sequence of values (such as lists, tuples or a strings) and execute the indented block of code multiple times, once for each element in the specified sequence.

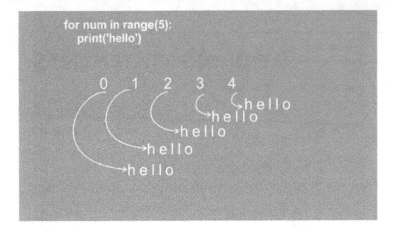

```
for num in range(5):
    print('hello')
```

0 1 2 3 4
hello
hello
hello
hello
hello

The basic syntax of a for loop in Python is as follows:

for variable in sequence:
        # execute this block of code

In a for loop, the variable that comes after the for keyword is linked to the first item in a sequence. The code block within the loop is executed, and then the variable is linked to the next item in the sequence.

This process continues until the loop reaches the end of the sequence, allowing the code block to be executed for each item in the sequence one at a time.

```
nums = [1,2,3,4,5]
for num in nums:
    print(num)
```

Output:
1
2
3
4

In this example, the for loop iterates through the list, associating num with each item in sequence, and printing it.

In addition to numbers, the for loop allows you to iterate over various types of sequences.

You can use the for loop to iterate over any kind of sequence, such as lists, strings, tuples, or even custom sequences you create.

```
fruits = ['apple', 'orange', 'pineapple', 'strawberry', 'grape']
for fruit in fruits:
    print(fruit)
```

Output:

apple

orange

pineapple

strawberry

grape

Apart from using a predefined list, you can use the built-in range() function to generate a sequence of numbers to iterate over.

The range() function

The range() function is used to generate a sequence of numbers within a specified range. The basic syntax is as follows:

range(start, stop, step)

> **Pro Tip:**
> *The start is the initial value of the sequence. It is optional and defaults to 0 when not provided. The stop is the end value of the sequence. The sequence will encompass all numbers starting from the provided start value up to, but not including, the stop value. Then, the step is the size or interval between numbers in the sequence. If not provided, it will default to 1.*

Here is an example to illustrate the usage:

```
#using range() function
for num in range(5):
    print(num)
```

Output:

0
1
2
3

While loop

The while loop allows you to repeatedly execute a block of code as long as a certain condition is true. It begins with a condition. If the condition evaluates to True, the block of codes under it is executed.The process is repeated like this as long as the test keeps evaluating to True.

The while loop consists of the while keyword, followed by a conditional test and a colon. The next line is an indented block of code. This block of code only executes if the test condition is True.

The loop keeps going until the condition is no longer true. Once that condition becomes false, the program stops looping and moves on to the next set of instructions.

The syntax of a while loop in Python is:

while condition:
  statement(s)

> **Pro Tip:**
> *If the condition never becomes false or if there's no mechanism to break out of the loop, the program will get stuck in an infinite loop, endlessly repeating the same set of instructions. This can lead to the program becoming unresponsive and consuming a lot of resources, which is something we want to avoid in programming. This can be achieved by including statements inside the loop that modify the loop condition.*

Now, let's use the while loop to print numbers ranging from 0 to 9:

```
count = 0
while count < 10:
    print(count)
    count += 1
```

Output:
0
1
2
3
4
5
6
7
8
9

In the above example, the variable "count" is initialized with a value of 0. The while loop is defined with the condition that it will iterate as long as "count" is less than 10.

Inside the loop, the current value of "count" is printed using the statement print(count). The "count" is incremented by 1 with each iteration.

Consequently, the loop persists until the value of "count" reaches 10, at which point the condition becomes false, leading to the termination of the loop.

Jump statements

Jump statements are used to control the flow of execution within a program by altering the order in which statements are executed. These statements allow you to transfer control to a different part of the code based on certain conditions.

The most common jump statements in Python are:

- Break
- Continue
- Pass

Break

The break statement is used to terminate the execution of a loop prematurely. It is typically used inside a for or while loop to exit the loop before the loop has finished iterating through all of its elements.

When the break statement is encountered within a loop, the loop is immediately exited and control is transferred to the statement immediately following the loop.

Below is an example that demonstrates the usage of the break statement in a for loop to end the loop when a specific condition is satisfied:

```python
#break example
for num in range(10):
    if num > 5:
        break
    print(num)
```

Output:
0
1
2
3
4
5

In the above example, the program iterates through the values in the range until it encounters a number greater than 5. At that point, the loop will be terminated by the break statement.

Continue

The continue statement allows you to skip the current iteration of the loop and move directly to the next one. When the continue statement is encountered, the loop takes a leap forward to the next iteration, bypassing any remaining code within the current iteration.

Here is an example of using the continue statement within a for loop:

```python
#continue example
for num in range(10):
    if num == 5:
        continue
    print(num)
```

Output:

0
1
2
3
4
6
7
8
9

In this example, the for loop is used to iterate over the numbers in the range from 0 to 9. When the number 5 is encountered, it is skipped and the loop continues with the next number. As a result, the code will print all the numbers from 0 to 4 and 6 to 9, excluding the number 5.

Pass

The pass statement is a null operation. It simply does nothing and is often used as a placeholder for code that has not been implemented yet or for code that will be implemented later.

Here is an example of using pass in an if statement:

```
for num in range(10):
    pass
```

Summary

In this chapter, you learnt how to use the for loop and while loop to execute codes repeatedly. The for loop allows you to iterate over a sequence (such as a list, tuple, or string) or any kind of sequence. The while loop repeatedly executes a block of code as long as a specified condition is true. You learnt how to use the continue and break statements to skip or exit the loop prematurely.

Practice Exercises

1. Explain the concept of looping in programming?

2. State the two types of looping constructs in Python.
3. Explain the range() function.
4. Write a program using the for loop to display the word "hello" 10 times
5. Write a program to print numbers from 1 to 10 and their squares using the while and for loops.
6. Write a program to determine the last digit of a number.
7. Write a number that determines if a number is a perfect square.
8. Write a program that takes a sequence of number and check if all numbers are unique.
9. Write a program to accept numbers from 1 to 7 and display them as Sunday, Monday and so on.
10. Write a program that displays a multiplication table.
11. Write a program that prints a table of binary, octal, decimal and hexadecimal equivalents for 1 to 256.
12. Write a program that counts the number of digits in a number.
13. Write a program that prompts the user for 5 numbers and prints the numbers in a line and each number separated by 4 whitespaces.
14. Write a program that reads numbers and displays the smallest and the largest numbers.
15. Write a program that prints the summation of all the numbers from 1 to 100.
16. Calculate the LCM and HCF of two numbers using python.
17. Write a number guessing game.

## Chapter 6

STRINGS

"I like to combine the dramatic emotional warmth of strings with the grooves and body business of drums and bass."
- David Byrne

Every single program we write is actually made up of characters, like alphabets, numbers, and symbols. No matter the complexity of a program, it all comes down to the fundamental elements. They are the raw materials we use to construct our code. It's remarkable how these characters can be combined in various ways to create meaningful statements, words, and sentences within our programs. They give us the power to communicate instructions and logic to the computer. And when we have a group of characters that are treated as a single unit, like a phrase or a sentence, we call it a string.

Learning outcome

In this chapter, you will learn:
- What strings are and how they are used to represent text.
- String manipulation operations like concatenation, slicing, and repetition.
- Different methods of formatting strings.
- To use the built-in string methods to perform common string operations.

Introduction

Strings are used to represent a collection of characters. You can create a string by enclosing the characters within either single (") or double ("") quotation marks.

Strings are immutable, which means that once a string is created, its content cannot be modified. This means that you cannot change individual characters within a string after it has been created.

Creating a String

To create a string in Python, simply enclose a sequence of characters in quotes.

```
country = 'Algeria'
sentence = 'How are you?'
```

Pro Tip:
It is important to note that in Python, single and double quotes can be used interchangeably to create a string, as long as they match.

Operations on strings

Python provides a variety of operations and methods to work with strings. Here are some commonly used operations on strings:

- Concatenation
- Repetitions
- Indexing
- Slicing
- Looping

Concatenation

Concatenation is the process of combining or joining two or more strings together to create a new string. It allows you to merge the contents of multiple strings into a single string.

When you use the + operator between two strings, it joins the characters of the strings in the order they appear, producing a new string that contains the combined characters.

For example:

```
#concatenation of strings
str1 = 'ice'
str2 = 'cream'

result = str1 + str2
print(result)
```

Output:
Icecream

If you want to put a space in between the words, you can include a white space as shown below:

```
#include a white space
result = str1 + "" + str2
```

```
print(result)
```

Output:
ice cream

Repetitions

To repeat a string, you simply write the string followed by the asterisk symbol (*) and then the number of times you want the string to be repeated.

> **Pro Tip:**
> *Normally, this operator does multiplication with numbers, but when it comes to strings, it does something different. It actually repeats the string as many times as you specify.*

```
#repetition of strings
greeting = 'hello!'
result = greeting * 3
print(result)
```

Output:
hello!hello!hello!

Indexing

You can access individual characters or a range of characters within a string by their position. In Python, strings are zero-indexed, which means the first character of a string is at index 0, the second character is at index 1, and so on.

To access a specific character in a string, you can use square brackets [] with the index value inside.

```
#indexing in strings
fruit = 'apple'
print(fruit[0])
print(fruit[1])
print(fruit[2])
print(fruit[3])
print(fruit[4])
```

Output:

a

p

p

l

e

You can also use negative indexing to access characters from the end of the string. The index -1 represents the last character, -2 represents the second-to-last character, and so on.

```
#negative indexing
fruit = 'apple'
print(fruit[-1])
print(fruit[-2])
print(fruit[-3])
print(fruit[-4])
print(fruit[-5])
```

Output:

e

l

p

p

a

Also, strings are immutable, meaning that you cannot perform remove or update characters in a string once it has been defined, else you will get an error.

For instance:

```
color = 'yellow'
color[0] = 'Y'
```

Output:

TypeError: 'str' object does not support item assignment

Slicing

Slicing enables you to extract a specific portion or substring from a string. It allows you to create a new string containing a range of characters from the original string.

While indexing involves fetching a specific character from a string based on its position or index, slicing involves extracting a range of characters from a string.

To perform slicing, you use square brackets []. Inside these brackets, you specify the start and end index of the desired substring separated by a colon (:).

```
#slicing a string
result = fruit[1:3]
print(result)
```

Output:
pp

> **Pro Tip:**
> *When you slice a string, the start index is inclusive, meaning it includes the character at that index. The end index, however, is exclusive, so it does not include the character at that index.*

Slicing can also include additional parameters, such as step size, which determines the increment between indices in the slice. The default step size is 1, but you can specify a different value to skip elements.

Here's an example that demonstrates slicing with a step size:

```
#slicing with step
fruit = 'pineapple'
result = fruit[0:10:2]
print(result)
```

Output:
Pnape

Looping a string

Strings are considered as sequences of characters. This characteristic allows you to iterate through each individual character in a string using either a for loop or a while loop.

```
for char in 'apple':
    print(char)
```

Output:

a

p

p

l

e

Built-in methods for string

Python has a variety of built-in methods that can be used to manipulate strings. Here are some commonly used built-in methods for strings:

- **lower():** Converts all characters in a string to lowercase.
- **upper():** Converts all characters in a string to uppercase.
- **capitalize():** Capitalizes the first character of a string.
- **strip():** Removes leading and trailing whitespace from a string.
- **split():** Splits a string into a list of substrings based on a specified separator.
- **join():** Joins a list of strings into a single string using a specified separator.
- **isdigit():** Checks if all characters in a string are digits.
- **isalpha():** Checks if all characters in a string are alphabetic.
- **islower():** Checks if all characters in a string are lowercase.
- **isupper():** Checks if all characters in a string are uppercase.

Take a look at the following example:

```
name = 'John'

#lower
print(name.lower())
```

```python
#upper
print(name.upper())

#capitalize
print(name.capitalize())

#title
sentence = 'how are you doing?'
print(sentence.title())

#strip
word = '  hello '
print(word.strip())

#split
sentence = 'how are you doing?'
print(sentence.split())

#join
words = ' '.join(['hello', 'there'])
print(words)

#isdigit
nums = '1234'
print(nums.isdigit())

nums = '12 Hillview'
print(nums.isdigit())

#isalpha
word = 'hello'
print(word.isalpha())

nums = '1234'
print(nums.isalpha())

#islower
word = 'hello'
print(word.islower())

word = 'HELLO'
```

```
print(word.islower())

#isupper
word = 'hello'
print(word.isupper())

word = 'HELLO'
print(word.isupper())
```

Output:
john
JOHN
John
How Are You Doing?
hello
['how', 'are', 'you', 'doing?']
hello there
True
False
True
False
True
False
False
True

Membership Test

Strings supports membership tests. Using the in operator, you can determine whether a character or group of characters are in a given string. The outcome of this operation is either True or False.

```
color = 'yellow'
print('y' in color)
print('llo' in color)
print('x' in color)
```

Outputs:
True
True
False

Triple quotes

Triple quotes also known as docstrings are used to create multiline strings. Even though some consider this as a way of commenting strings, but technically, docstrings or characters in triple quotes are considered as strings.

> **Pro Tip:**
> *You can use triple single or double quotes, but be consistent in your choice, otherwise you will get a syntax error. However, it's recommended that you only use single or double quotes in defining strings. Triple quotes are predominantly used for code documentations. Also, avoid using triple quotes for the commenting except if it is part of your program documentations.*

```
"""
This is the documentation for the program
"""
#triple quotes used in defining strings
S = """Hello 1"""
print(S)
S = '''hello 2'''
print(S)
S = '''Wrong"""
```

Outputs:
Hello 1
hello 2

SyntaxError: unterminated triple-quoted string literal (detected at line 17)

Strings and built-in functions

Python has a rich set of built-in functions that can be used to manipulate and process strings. Some commonly used built-in functions for strings in Python are:

* len()
* str()
* ord()

len()

The len() function is a built-in function that returns the length or the number of items in a sequence. When used with strings, it returns the number of characters in the string.

So, the length of a string is essentially the same thing as the number of characters within that string.

```
fruit = 'grape'
print(len(fruit))
```

Output:
5

str()

The str() function is a built-in function that converts an object into a string representation. It can be used with various data types, including numbers, booleans, lists, tuples, and more.

Also, it provides a convenient way to convert non-string objects into string format, making them suitable for string manipulation and display purposes.

```
#using str() function to convert integer to string
num = 1200
result = str(num)
print(num)
```

Output:
1200

ord()

Each character is represented in Unicode using a unique value called a code point. There may be instances where you need to find the Unicode code point of a specific character, and that's when the ord() function comes in handy.

By using the ord() function, you can easily determine the Unicode code point associated with a particular character.

```
#using ord to get unicode code points
print(ord('h'))
print(ord('p'))
print(ord('.'))
```

Output:
104
112
46

Escape characters

Escape characters are special characters that are used to represent non-printable characters or to create special characters within string literals. They allow you to use characters that are hard to represent in a string.

When Python encounters escape characters, it interprets it as a special character rather than as part of the string. They are represented by a backslash (\) followed by a character or a sequence of characters.

Here are a few examples of commonly used escape characters in Python:

- \n- newline character
- \t- tab character
- \\- backslash character
- \"- double quote character
- \'- single quote character
- \b- backspace character
- \r- carriage return character
- \f- formfeed character

Let's explore some examples that involve the use of escape characters.

```
#escape characters example
str1 = 'hello \tthere'
print(str1)
```

```
str2 = 'hello \nthere'
print(str2)

str3 = 'This is a string with a newline character\nand a tab
character\tin it.'
print(str3)
```

Output:
hello   there
hello
there
This is a string with a newline character
and a tab character   in it.

In this example, the escape characters \n and \t are used to create a new line and a tab within the string.

Raw strings

A regular string is represented as a sequence of characters enclosed within single (' ') or double (" ") quotes. However, in certain situations, the presence of escape characters can lead to unintended outcomes.

For instance, if you want to include a quotation mark within a string, you use an escape character like this:

```
"He said, \"Hello!\""
```

Here, the backslash before the second double quote tells the interpreter to treat it as a regular character, not the end of the string.

Now, if you want to make the compiler ignore escape characters and treat a string the way it is, you can use a raw string.

To create a raw string, simply place an 'r' before the beginning quotation mark. By using a raw string, all escape characters within the string will be completely ignored, and any backslashes present will be printed as they are without any special interpretation.

```
#raw string
str1 = r'hello \nthere'
print(str1)
```

Output:
hello \nthere

String substitution methods

String substitution plays a significant role when it comes to manipulating strings in Python. It allows you to create dynamic strings by incorporating variables, expressions, or other strings into a larger string.

Python provides various methods for performing string substitutions, including the following:

- Format function
- F-strings
- Old string substitution

Format function

The format() function in Python is a built-in method for strings that allows you to perform string formatting and substitution.

To use this function, you are required to include curly braces {} as placeholders in your string. These curly braces act like markers that tell the function where you want to perform substitutions.

Inside the curly braces, you can specify the positions or even assign names to the values or variables you want to substitute.

```
S = '{} shirts in the {} box'.format(5, 'blue')
print(S)
```

Outputs:
5 shirts in the blue box

The above example contains two placeholders enclosed in curly braces. These placeholders serve as markers, indicating the positions in the string where the values will be inserted or substituted.

By calling the format() function, the placeholders in the string are replaced with the provided values. The resulting string is then assigned to the variable S. In this case, the value of S would be '5 shirts in the blue box'.

In addition, if you want to have more control over the substitution process and not rely solely on the positions of the arguments in the format() function, you can include numbers within the curly braces.

This allows you to specify explicitly which value should be substituted at each placeholder.

```
S = '{0} shirts in the {1} box'.format(5, 'blue')
print(S)
```

Outputs:
5 shirts in the blue box

Now, if you want to switch things up and have the first argument replace the second set of curly braces, while the second argument takes the place of the first set of curly braces, you can achieve that by assigning a higher number to the first set of curly braces compared to the second set.

```
S = '{1} shirts in the {0} box'.format(5, 'blue')
print(S)
```

Outputs:
blue shirts in the 5 box

F-strings

F-strings also known as formatted string literals is an easy way to perform string substitution in python. Instead of using the format() function or concatenation, you can place the variables or expressions directly inside curly braces {} within the string.

To use f-strings for string substitution, you simply need to include the letter 'f' before the opening quotation mark of a string. This signals that the string is an f-string. Inside the f-string, you can place expressions or variables within curly braces {}.

These expressions are treated as valid Python expressions and will be evaluated and substituted with their corresponding values when the string is evaluated.

```
box = 'blue'
S = f'There are {2+3} shirts in the {box} box'
print(S)
```

The above example contains two placeholders enclosed in curly braces {}. The first placeholder {2+3} contains an expression 2+3, which evaluates to 5. The second placeholder {box} expects the value of the variable 'box' to be substituted.

So, when the f-string is evaluated, the curly braces and the expression inside them will be replaced by the computed value, resulting in the string below:

Output:
There are 5 shirts in the blue box

Old String Substitution

This involves the use of the % operator for substitution. To use the % operator for string substitution, you start with a string containing one or more placeholders represented by %s. These placeholders act as slots where values will be inserted.

```
S = '%s oranges' % 5
print(S)
```

Output:
5 oranges

In the above example, the character after the % operator is substituted by the argument provided at the end of the string, and in this case 5.

However, if more than one substitution is to be performed, the arguments for substitution should be enclosed in a parenthesis as shown below.

```
S = '%s shirts in the %s box' % (5, 'blue')
print(S)
```

Output:
5 oranges

Standard string formatting specifiers

Python provides a powerful way for presenting data in a clear and organized format through its standard string formatting specifiers. These specifiers provide a structured way to create formatted strings.

Here is the syntax:

[[fill]align][sign][#][0][minimumwidth][.precision][type]

Type

The type indicates the type of data that is expected or how the data should be presented.

String type - s

Numeric types
- 'b' binary
- 'c' character
- 'd' decimal integer
- 'o' octal
- 'x' hexadecimal
- 'X' hexadecimal
- 'n' number
- ' ' none

Take a look at this example:

```
S = 'Hello there %s' % 5
print(S)

S = 'Hello there %s' % '5'
print(S)
S = 'Hello there %d' % 5
print(S)
S = 'Hello there %f' % 5
print(S)
S = 'Hello there %c' % '5'
print(S)
```

Outputs:

Hello there 5
Hello there 5
Hello there 5
Hello there 5.000000
Hello there 5

Floating point types

- 'e' exponent
- 'E' exponent
- 'f' fixed point
- 'F' fixed point
- 'g' general
- 'G' general
- 'n' number
- '%' percentage

Time types

- 'a' - abbreviated weekday name
- 'A' - full weekday Name
- 'b' - abbreviated month name
- 'B' - full month name
- 'd' - day
- 'H' - hour with trailing zeros
- 'M' - Minutes with trailing zeros
- 'S' - Seconds with trailing zeros
- 'Y' - year with century

Precision

This is a decimal number indicating number of digits after the decimal point. It is predominantly used if the expected argument is a float.

```
S = 'Hello there %.2f' % 5
print(S)
S = 'Hello there %.5f' % 5
print(S)
```

Outputs:

Hello there 5.00

Hello there 5.00000

Width

This is a decimal number indicating the minimum field width. If the width argument is less than the width, then you may decide to pad the characters of your choice.

```
S = '%d oranges' % 5
print(S)
S = '%5d oranges' % 5
print(S)
S = '%05d oranges' % 5
print(S)
S = '%10s oranges' % 'apple'
print(S)
```

Outputs:
5 oranges
        5 oranges
00005 oranges
        apple oranges

Fill

The fill is used to indicate the character to be used to pad the field to minimum width as shown below:

```
S = '%05d oranges' % 5
print(S)
```

Outputs:
00005 oranges

Summary

In this chapter, you learnt concept of strings and how they are used to represent text in Python. You performed various string manipulation operations such as concatenation, slicing, and repetition. You learnt the different techniques for formatting strings and embedding variables and expressions within a string. You also learnt about the numerous built-in string methods for performing common operations like splitting, and joining strings.

Practice Exercises

1. How do you define a string in Python?
2. String is an immutable object, what does it mean?
3. Write a program to combine two strings together to form another string.
4. Write a program to determine the length of a string.
5. Write a program that counts the number of the individual characters in a string.
6. Write a program to get the nth item in a non empty string.
7. Write a program that reverses a string
8. Explain split and join methods of strings.
9. Write a program to convert a tuple to a string
10. Write a program that displays the ASCII number and the corresponding characters.
11. Write a program that generates random passwords containing alphabets, numbers and symbols.
12. Write a program that removes vowels from a word.

## Chapter 7

LISTS

"The human animal differs from the lesser primates in his passion for lists."
- H. Allen Smith

Let's say you want to go shopping. To ensure you don't forget anything, you start by making a list of items you need to buy. With pen and paper, you can start writing down or listing the items you need to purchase. You may want to review and revise your shopping list from time to time. You may wish to remove some items you considered not essential or add new ones that you remember. Also, you iterate over your shopping list, making adjustments to ensure it reflects your needs accurately. You may decide to arrange the items on your shopping list based on their importance or priority. And just like your shopping list, a list in python is a collection of items.

Learning outcome

In this chapter, you will learn:
- To use lists to store items.
- To access, retrieve and modify items in a list.
- To Sort or arrange the items in a list.
- To Iterate through the items in a list.
- How to create lists on the fly using list comprehension.

Introduction

When it comes to managing collections of data in Python, one of the most versatile and fundamental data structures is the list.

Lists can hold items of different data types and are created by enclosing items or objects in a square bracket, with each item separated by a comma.

```
L = [1,2,3,4,5]
```

An empty list is represented by a pair of square brackets with nothing in-between:

```
L = [ ]
```

Lists are mutable, meaning that they can be modified after creation and serve as versatile containers capable of storing a diverse range of data items, including items of different types.

This means that you can store items of different data types such as numbers, strings and even lists or other data types in the same list.

```
#heterogeneous list
L = ['age', 2.34, True, 250]
```

Also, lists can be nested, which means you can have lists within lists, forming a matrix or a multi-dimensional structure. This nesting capability allows you to create complex data structures where each element of the outer list can contain its own list.

```
#using list to form a matrix
L = [[1,2,3], [4,5,6], [7,8,9], [10,11,12]]
```

Indexing

You can access individual items by using their index. So, if you have a list with 5 items, the first item's index is 0, the second item's index is 1, and so on. The index of the last item in the list is always one less than the total number of items in the list. Hence, if you have 5 items, the last item's index is 4.

```
#indexing in lists
colours = ['orange', 'purple', 'green', 'red', 'brown']
print(colours[0])
print(colours[1])
print(colours[2])
print(colours[3])
print(colours[4])
```

Output:
orange
purple
green
red

brown

Pro Tip:
The index of the last item in the list will be n-1, where n represents the total number of items present in the list. So, if you have a list with 5 items, the indices would range from 0 to 4.

In above example, items in the list were accessed using positive indexes. However, you can also use negative indexes to do the same thing!

Instead of starting from 0 like in positive indexes, negative indexes start counting from the end of the list.

```
#negative indexes
print(colours[-1])
print(colours[-2])
print(colours[-3])
print(colours[-4])
print(colours[-5])
```

Output:
brown
red
green
purple
orange

Slicing

Slicing allows you to extract or fetch either specific items or a range of items from a list.

The syntax to slice a list looks like this:

List[start : end]

This will return all the items starting from the item with the index "start" and stopping but excluding the item with the index "end".

```
#slicing a list
result = colours[1:4]
```

```
print(result)
```

Output:
['purple', 'green', 'red']

Now, let's say you want to slice a list, but instead of grabbing all the items within a range, you actually want to skip or leave out some of them.

By adding an extra component to the slicing syntax, called the "step" value, you can specify how many items to skip between each item you want to include in the slice.

This way, you have full control over which items to include or exclude.

Take a look at this list:

```
L = [1,2,3,4,5,6,7,8,9,10]
```

To extract a portion of this list, beginning from index 4 and extending up to the last item with index 9, you can use the following syntax:

```
L[4:10]
```

Output:
[5, 6, 7, 8, 9, 10]

However, if you want to skip the item right after a selected index, or maybe you want to select every second item in the list, then you will include a step value as shown below:

```
L[4:10:2]
```

Output:
[5, 7, 9]

Adding items to a list

To add an item to an empty list or a list with an already existing item. The following methods are used:

- append()
- insert()

Append() method

The append() method serves to insert or add a specified item at the end of a list. It modifies the list in place and does not return a new list.

> **Pro Tip:**
> *Modifying a list in place means changing the contents of the existing list without creating a new list. When you modify a list in place, you are directly altering the original list object rather than creating a new one.*

In the example below, the append method is used to add items to an empty list.

```
L = []
L.append(1)
print(L)
L.append(2)
print(L)
L.append(4)
print(L)
```

Output:
[1]
[1, 2]
[1, 2, 4]

Insert() method

The insert() method in provides a way to add items to a list at any desired position, rather than just adding them as the last items. You are required to provide the item and index where the item will be added to the list.

```
fruits = ['orange', 'apple', 'grape']

fruits.insert(1, 'strawberry')
print(fruits)
```

In the above example, the item "strawberry" was added to the list at the index of 1.

Output:
['orange', 'strawberry', 'apple', 'grape']

Removing items from a list

When it comes to removing items from a list, you have two methods at your disposal and they include:

- pop()
- remove()

Let's take a closer look at each of them.

The pop() method

This is used to remove and return an element from a list based on its index. Aside from removing items from a list, the pop() method returns the item removed from the list as shown below:

> **Pro Tip:**
> *If you want to specifically remove the last item in a list, you can simply call pop() without providing any arguments.*

```
#pop method
fruits = ['orange', 'strawberry', 'apple', 'grape']
fruit = fruits.pop()

print(fruits)
print(fruit)
```

Output:
['orange', 'strawberry', 'apple']
grape

In the above example, the pop() method was used to remove the last element from a list and retrieve its value at the same time.

However, if you want to remove an item in a given position, you can provide the index as the argument to the pop method.

```
#pop method with argument
fruits = ['orange', 'strawberry', 'apple', 'grape']
fruit = fruits.pop(2)

print(fruits)
```

Output:
['orange', 'strawberry', 'grape']

Remove() method

The remove() method is used to remove the first occurrence of a given item in a list. To remove the first occurrence of a specific item from a list using the remove() method, you need to provide an argument that corresponds to the item you wish to remove.

```
#remove method
fruits = ['orange', 'strawberry', 'apple', 'grape']
fruits.remove('apple')
print(fruits)
```

Output:
['orange', 'strawberry', 'grape']

Sorting a list

Sorting is the process of organizing items in a particular order. Consider having a list of numbers or words, and the goal is to arrange them in a specific sequence. A lot of times, the purpose is to facilitate easy location, access, or analysis of items within the list.

Sorting can be accomplished using either the sort() method or the sorted() function on the list.

The sort() method

The sort() method allows you to sort the items in a list in ascending or descending order.

```
#sorting a list
fruits = ['orange', 'strawberry', 'apple', 'grape']
fruits.sort()
print(fruits)
```

Output:
['apple', 'grape', 'orange', 'strawberry']

The sort() method has an argument "reverse " which by default is set to False. This way, items are sorted in ascending order.

You can as well sort the items in descending order using the sort method. But, you have to set reverse to True.

```
fruits.sort(reverse=True)
print(fruits)
```

Output:
['strawberry', 'orange', 'grape', 'apple']

The sorted() Method

This method takes a list as an argument and returns a new list with the items sorted.

```
#sorted method

fruits = ['orange', 'strawberry', 'apple', 'grape']
result = sorted(fruits)
print(result)
```

Output:
['apple', 'grape', 'orange', 'strawberry']

Concatenation

Concatenation refers to the process of combining or joining two or more lists together to create a single, larger list. This can be achieved using the concatenation operator +.

Here's an example to illustrate the concept:

```
#concatenation of lists
L1 = [1,2,3,4]
L2 = [6,7,5]
result = L1 + L2
print(result)
```

Output:
[1, 2, 3, 4, 6, 7, 5]

List comprehension

List comprehension provides a mechanism to create a new list out of another list using a single line of code. It provides a concise and efficient way to perform operations on each element of a list and create a new list based on the results.

Let's say that you want to create a list containing the squares of the numbers in another list.

```
nums = [1,2,3,4,5]
squares = [num**2 for num in nums]
print(squares)
```

Output:
[1, 4, 9, 16, 25]

As simple as it looks, list comprehension can be used to perform powerful operations on sequences.

> **Pro Tip:**
> *The primary goal of list comprehension is to create straightforward and readable code. Overusing it can lead to complexity, undermining the very essence of simplicity and clarity that list comprehension aims to achieve.*

Applying conditionals in a list comprehension

List comprehension allows you to create list easily. It also allows you to use conditional logics ("if" and "else " conditionals) to alter the outcome of the newly created list.

For instance, you can use the list comprehension to create a list containing only even numbers from another list.

```
L = [1,2,3,4,5,6,7,8,9,10]
numbers = [num for num in L if num % 2 == 0]
print(numbers)
```

Output:
[2, 4, 6, 8, 10]

Similarly, you can create a new list containing only odd numbers, as shown below:

```
numbers = [num for num in L if num % 2 != 0]
print(numbers)
```

Output:
[1, 3, 5, 7, 9]

Also, you can also use list comprehension to create a list of all the characters in a given string.

```
chars = [char for char in 'hello']
print(chars)
```

Output:
['h', 'e', 'l', 'l', 'o']

You can also decide to filter out values from the new list as shown below:

```
result  = [num*2 for num in range(4) if num > 1]
print(result)
```

Output:
[4, 6]

Using list comprehension to create nested lists

Let's say that you want to create a list containing numbers and their respective square. You can easily do this with list comprehension as shown below:

```
L = [1,2,3,4,5]
squares = [[num, num**2] for num in L]
print(squares)
```

Output:
[[1, 1], [2, 4], [3, 9], [4, 16], [5, 25]]

Nested comprehension

A nested comprehension has a comprehension inside another comprehension. This allows you to create more complex lists or matrices in a concise and readable way.

For example:

```
L = [[1,2], [3,4], [5,6]]
result = [[x[i] for x in L] for i in range(2)]
print(result)
```

Output:
[[1, 3, 5], [2, 4, 6]]

The above example uses a nested list comprehension to transform the original list, creating a new list named result. The outer comprehension iterates over the range from 0 to 2, representing the indices of the sublists. For each index i, the inner comprehension extracts the i-th element from each sublist in L, effectively transforming the rows and columns of the original list.

map(), zip() and filter() functions

You can utilize in-built functions like map, zip and filter in a list comprehension to achieve even more sophisticated outcomes.

map() function

This is how the map function works. It performs a given action on all the elements of an iterable and returns the result as an iterable.

> **Pro Tip:**
> *An iterable is something you can iterate over, or in simpler terms, it's something that you can loop through. It's like a container holding multiple items, and you can go through each item one by one. Common examples of iterables include lists, strings, and tuples.*

Let's say that you want to square all the items in a list, the map() function requires that you provide a function that will perform the squares, and the list upon which the items will be squared.

To demonstrate this, let's use of the in-built trunc() function to remove all the decimal parts of numbers in a list.

```
L = [1.2,2.88,3.01,4.00,5.75]
num = map(trunc, L)
print(num)
```

Output:
[1, 2, 3, 4, 5]

Also, you can use the map() function alongside the abs() function to remove all the negative in numbers in a list.

```
num = map(abs, [-1,-2,-3,-4])
print(num)
```

Output:
[1, 2, 3, 4]

Map with user-defined functions

Apart from the standard in-built functions, you can also use custom defined functions with map.

Let's create a function that computes the square of any number.

```python
def square(num):
    return num**2
L = [1,2,3,4,5]
squares = map(square, L)
print(squares)
```

Output:
[1, 4, 9, 16, 25]

Apart from the regular functions, you can also use lambda functions with map function.

Using lambda functions with map

Lambda function is simply a function without name or rather an anonyous function. It's a way of creating function on the fly without the need for defining and calling on a function.

To use a lamba function in a map, simply use the lambda function in place of the argument for function in the map.

```python
L = [1,2,3,4,5]
squares = map(lambda num: num**2, L)
print(squares)
```

Using map with list comprehensions

Now, let's explore how the map function can be utilized in conjunction with list comprehension. The example below combined the functionalities of both the map and list comprehension to create a list of squares of items from another list.

```python
def square(num):
    return num**2
L = [1,2,3,4,5]
result = [num for num in map(square, L)]
print(result)
```

Output:
[1, 4, 9, 16, 25]

Athough, the above outcome can be achieved with only list comprehension alone, but the essence is to show you the both can be used to accomplish sophisticated results.

zip() function

The zip() function combines items from two or more lists into a list of tuples. These tuples are formed by pairing items located at the corresponding indices in the original lists. The first element of the tuple comes from the first list, the second element from the second list, and so on.

```
L1 = [1,2,3]
L2 = [4,5,6]
result = zip(L1, L2)
print(result)
```

Output:
[(1, 4), (2, 5), (3, 6)]

You can combine as many lists as possible using the zip() function as shown below:

```
L1 = [1,2,3]
L2 = [4,5,6]
L3 = [7,8,9]
L4 = [10,11,12]

result = zip(L1, L2, L3, L4)
print(result)
```

Output:
[(1, 4, 7, 10), (2, 5, 8, 11), (3, 6, 9, 12)]

Combining lists of variable lengths with zip

You can combine lists of different length with the zip function. However, the new list will have a length as that of the shortest list being zipped.

Hence, items in positions greater than that in the last item in the shortest list will be ignored or not be included in the new list.

```
L1 = [1,2,3]
L2 = [4,5]
L3 = [7,8,9]
result = zip(L1, L2, L3)
print(result)
```

Output:
[(1, 4, 7), (2, 5, 8)]

Now, let's use create a list using the list comprhensioin and the zip() function.

```
L1 = [1,2,3]
L2 = [4,5,6]
result = [x for x in zip(L1, L2)]
print(result)
```

Output:
[(1, 4), (2, 5), (3, 6)]

Supposed you want the newly created list to contain list of zip items instead of tuples, below will give you that outcome.

```
result = [[x,y] for [x,y] in zip(L1, L2)]
print(result)
```

Output:
[[1, 4], [2, 5], [3, 6]]

Now, let's make use the map() and zip() in a list comprehension to create something powerful.

We will be combining two lists together using the zip() function and then use the map() function to sum the elements in the respective tuples in the newly created list.

```
L1 = [1,2,3]
L2 = [4,5,6]
result = [num**2 for num in map(sum, zip([1,2,3], [2,3,4]))]
print(result)
```

Output:
[9, 25, 49]

filter() function

The filter function just like the map() function requires a function as an argument. The map() function iterates over all the items in the iterable and at the same time performing a function call using the items as an argment and returning the result.

On the other hand, the filter() function performs conditional operations on the items in the iterable with the aim to return or retain the various items in the list being created.

For example, let's use the filter() function to create a list with all the items as even numbers.

```
L = [1,2,3,4,5,6,7,8,9,10]
def is_even(num):
        if num % 2 == 0:
        return True
result = filter(is_even, L)
print(result)
```

Output:
[2, 4, 6, 8, 10]

You can also use the lambda function as with the zip() function as shown below:

```
L = [1,2,3,4,5,6,7,8,9,10]
result = filter((lambda x: x % 2 == 0), L)
print(result)
```

Output:
[2, 4, 6, 8, 10]

Summary

This chapter started by explaining the concept of lists and how they are used to store collections of items in programming. You learnt how to create lists, access and modify their elements, sort them, iterate through their items, and even create lists on the fly using list comprehension.

Practice Exercises

1. How do you create a list in Python?
2. Explain negative indexing and their uses.
3. What is slicing in Python?
4. Write a program that determines the second largest number in a list.
5. Write a program that reverses a list.
6. Use list comprehension to construct a new list by adding 5 to individual items in the original list.
7. Explain with examples the uses of zip(), map() and filter() methods in list comprehensions.
8. Write a program to check and return the pairs of a given list whose sum is equal to the target value.

## Chapter 8

TUPLES

"Shakespeare did not consider himself the legislator of mankind. He faithfully records man's problems and does not evidently propose to solve them."
- Allan Bloom

Imagine that you are to write a list of items that you don't want to be tampered with. Maybe, a list of evidence from a crime scene or a list of patients' symptoms that shouldn't be altered. You wouldn't want anyone tampering with the list or accidentally modifying it. Well, that's where tuples come into play. Unlike lists, tuples are immutable, meaning once you create them, you can't modify or update them.

Learning outcome

In this chapter, you will learn:
- To create a tuple.
- To access and retrieve items within a tuple.
- The immutability of tuples.
- How to pack and unpack tuples.

Introduction

Tuples are similar to lists, but with one key difference: they are immutable, meaning their elements cannot be modified once created. Tuples are created using parentheses, with elements separated by commas. However, it's important to note that the use of parentheses is optional.

```
tup = (1,2,3,4,5)
```

An empty tuple is created with an empty parenthesis while a tuple with a single item is created by leaving a trailing comma after the item in the parenthesis.

```
#empty tuple
tup = ()
#tuple with single item
tup = (1,)
```

Packing and unpacking of tuples

In Python, packing refers to the process of combining multiple values or items into a single unit. It is a term used to describe the creation of a tuple by assigning values separated by commas to a variable without using the parenthesis.

For example:

```
T = 1,2,3,4,5
```

This is the same thing as:

```
T = (1,2,3,4,5)
```

> **Pro Tip:**
> *Creating a tuple is same thing as packing tuples.*

On the other hand, unpacking is a way of fetching the items in a tuple and assigning the values to variables. When you assign the individual values in a tuple to variables, you are unpacking the tuple.

```
a,b,c = 1,2,3

print(a)
print(b)
print(c)
```

Output:
1
2
3

The above example demonstrates the use of unpacking to assign values to multiple variables in a single line.

This means that you are allowed to unpack a tuple with a given number of items into variables corresponding to the total number of items in the tuple.

Unpacking when the list has more items than variables

Consider a situation where there are more items than the number of variables on the left side of the assignment. This creates a mismatch during tuple unpacking and results in an error because there are not enough variables to receive all the items in the tuple.

To avoid this error, you can use a starred expression (*) to capture the excess items into a single variable.

```
T = (1,2,3)
num1, *num2 = T
print(num1)
print(num2)
```

Output:
1
[2, 3]

In the above example, the variable num1 is assigned to 1 and the starred variable num2 takes the rest of the items in the tuple. However, if the num1 is starred, then num two becomes assigned to the last item on the tuple and num1 takes the rest of the items.

```
T = (1,2,3)
*num1, num2 = T
print(num1)
print(num2)
```

Output:
[1, 2]
3

Dummy variables

Dummy variables are used as placeholders and doesn't carry any meaningful information. A dummy variable is usually named with a single underscore (_) to indicate that its value is not going to be used.

Sometimes, you might have a tuple with more values than you need, and you're only interested in extracting specific items. Instead of creating unnecessary variables for the values you don't need, you can use a dummy variable to skip those values during unpacking.

```
_,a,b = (1,2,3)
print(a)
```

```
_,a,b,_ = (1,2,3,4)
print(a)
print(b)
```

Output:

2

2

3

Operations on tuples

You can perform most of the operations of a list on a tuple. These operations include accessing individual elements by index, slicing, iteration, and checking the length of the tuple.

However, the key difference is that any operation involving the modification of items, such as adding, removing, or changing elements, is forbidden in tuples.

The following examples demonstrate indexing and slicing of tuples:

```
#indexing a tuple
tup = (1,2,3,4,5)
result = tup[2]
print(result)
#slicing a tuple
result = tup[1:3]
print(result)
```

Output:

3

(2, 3)

Immutability of Tuples

Tuples are immutable types and as such cannot be updated or modified. Trying to change or update the values of a tuple will result in an error.

```
#tuples are immutable
tup[1] = 3
```

Built-in functions on tuples

Python provides several built-in functions can be used to perform various operations on tuples. Here are some of the commonly used built-in functions for tuples:

len() function

The len() function is used to determine the length or number of items in a tuple.

```
T1 = (1,2,3)
T2 = ('green', 'yellow', 'blue', 'red', 'purple')
print(len(T1))
print(len(T2))
```

Output:
3
5

count() function

The count function is used to determine the number of a given item in a list. For instance, you can use the count() function to determine the number of occurrences of the item 2 in a tuple.

```
num = (1,2,3,4,4,3,1,2,5,7,2,5,2,1)
print(num.count(1))
print(num.count(2))
print(num.count(4))
```

Output:
3
4
2

min() and max() function

The min() and max() functions are used to determine the smallest or largest item in a tuple.

```
L = (1,2,3,4,4,3,1,2,5,7,2,5,2,1)
min_value = min(L)
max_value = max(L)
print(min_value)
print(max_value)
```

Output:
1
7

tuple() function

The tuple() function is used to convert a sequence into a tuple. The examples below use the tuple function to convert a string and a list into tuples.

```
str_value = 'hello'
list_value = ['orange', 'banana', 'grape']
print(tuple(str_value))
print(tuple(list_value))
```

Output:
('h', 'e', 'l', 'l', 'o')
('orange', 'banana', 'grape')

index() function

This function locates and returns the index of the first occurrence of a particular item within a tuple.

```
L = (1,2,3,4,4,3,1,2,5,7,2,5,2,1)
print(L.index(1))
print(L.index(2))
print(L.index(3))
print(L.index(7))
```

Output:
0

Differences between tuples and lists

Lists and tuples are very powerful data structures in python. Despite their substantial similarities, certain distinctions set them apart from each other. Here are highlights of some of the differences between tuples and lists.

List	Tuple
Mutable	Immutable
Items are enclosed in a square bracket	Items are enclosed in a parenthesis
Can be sorted	Cannot be sorted
Consumes more memory	Consumes less memory
Represents a field	Represents a record or row

Named Tuples

Namedtuple is a special kind of tuple that makes it possible to create immutable sequence that can be accessed based on their field names and dot notations. Instead of using the positional indices, values within the sequence are accessed using designated field names.

To create a namedtuple, you have to import the namedtuple function from the collections module.

```
from collections import namedtuple

numbers = namedtuple('number', ['a', 'b', 'c'])
even = numbers(2,4,6)
numbers(a=2, b=4, c=6)
for i in even:
    print(i)
```

Outputs:
2

4
6

Once a namedtuple is defined, values can be accessed using dot notation, as shown below

```
print(even.a)
print(even.b)
print(even.c)
print(even[2])
```

Outputs:
2
4
6
6

Summary

In this chapter, you learnt concept of tuples and how they are used to store collections of items in programming. Tuples are similar to lists except that they are immutable. This means that their elements cannot be modified once they are created. You learned how to create tuples, access and retrieve their items, understand their immutability, and work with packing and unpacking techniques.

Practice Exercises

1. Explain the concept of packing and unpacking of tuples.
2. Write a program to unpack a tuple in several variables.
3. How do you compare two tuples to see if they have the same elements?
4. How do you convert a tuple to a list?
5. Provide 5 differences between a tuple and a list.
6. What are the applications of tuples in real world?
7. Explain the immutability of tuples and its significance in the use of tuples as a data type.

Chapter 9

DICTIONARIES

"The only place success comes before work is in the dictionary."
- Vince Lombardi

Have you ever come across a word that you just don't understand the meaning? The easiest way to look for the meaning of a word, is by looking up the word in your dictionary. The word is like the key to the meaning that you seek. By proving the word, you can unlock the meaning. Interestingly, this concept is similar to Python dictionaries. However, instead of words and definitions, they store key-value pairs of items allowing you to represent and organize complex data.

Learning outcome

In this chapter, you will learn:
- What dictionaries are and how they differ from other data types.
- To create dictionaries?
- To access, modify or delete specific elements within a dictionary.
- The various built-in methods for dictionaries.
- To iterate over items in dictionaries.

Introduction

A dictionary is a collection of items comprising key-value pairs separated by commas and enclosed in a curly brace. It is also known as an associative array or a hash table in other programming languages.

Each key is matched with a corresponding value using a colon. The key is positioned on the left, and the value on the right. Every key must be unique and is linked to a specific value.

Values within dictionaries can be of any data type, including integers, strings, lists, or even other dictionaries. Key-value pairs are delimited by colons (:) and enclosed within curly braces ({ }).

Also, dictionaries are mutable, meaning you can modify them after they are created.

Hence, a dictionary is created by by enclosing key-value pairs within curly braces.

```
subjects = {1:'chemistry', 2:'history', 3:'government',
            4:'geography', 5:'mathematics' }
```

In the above dictionary, the keys are 1, 2, 3, 4 and 5, while the values are 'chemistry', 'history', 'government', 'geography' and 'mathematics'

To define an empty dictionary, you can simply provide empty curly braces.

```
#an empty dictionary
subjects = {}
```

Accessing values in a dictionary

You can access a value in a dictionary through its key. To do this, you either, use the slice operator [] or the get method of the dictionary.

```
#accessing items in a dictionary
subjects = {1:'chemistry', 2:'history', 3:'government',
            4:'geography', 5:'mathematics' }

#using slicing operator
subject = subjects[1]
print(subject)
```

Output:
chemistry

However, trying to access a value through a key that doesn't exist (using the slice operator) in the dictionary will result in a key error.

So, if you are unsure of the key, you can use the get() method as shown below:

```
#using get method
subject = subjects.get(3)
print(subject)
```
Output:

Government

Updating the values in a dictionary

Dictionaries are mutable and so, you can update or modify them. To do this, you can use the slice operator [] along with the corresponding key to modify or update the associated values.

```
#updating items in a dictionary
subjects[1] = 'agriculture'
print(subjects)
```

Output:
{1: 'agriculture', 2: 'history', 3: 'government', 4: 'geography', 5: 'mathematics'}

Adding items to a dictionary

You can add a new item to a dictionary by assigning value to a non-exiting key in the dictionary.

Take a look at this dictionary.

```
#adding a new item to dictionary
subjects = {1: 'agriculture', 2: 'history', 3: 'government', 4:
            'geography'}
```

You can add a new item by assigning the key 5, which is not present in the dictionary to a value.

```
subjects[5] = 'mathematics'
print(subjects)
```

Output:
{1: 'agriculture', 2: 'history', 3: 'government', 4: 'geography', 5: 'mathematics'}

Deleting items in a dictionary

While working with dictionaries, you might encounter situations where the removal of items becomes necessary. Deleting items from a dictionary can be achieved through various methods, and here are three commonly used approaches:

- del keyword
- pop() method
- popitem() method

The del statement

The most straightforward method to remove an item from a dictionary is by using the del statement. You can use this method to delete the entire dictionary or a specific item in a dictionary.

```
subjects = {1: 'agriculture', 2: 'history', 3: 'government', 4:
            'geography', 5: 'mathematics'}

del subjects[5]
print(subjects)
```

Output:
{1: 'agriculture', 2: 'history', 3: 'government', 4: 'geography'}

In the above example, the key 5 and its associated value are removed from the subjects dictionary using the del statement.

The pop() method

The pop() method allows you to remove and return the value associated with a specified key.

```
subjects = {1: 'agriculture', 2: 'history', 3: 'government', 4:
            'geography', 5: 'mathematics'}

subject = subjects.pop(2)
print(subject)
print(subjects)
```

Output:
history
{1: 'agriculture', 3: 'government', 4: 'geography', 5: 'mathematics'}

The popitem() method

The popitem() method is used to remove and return the last key-value pair from the dictionary as a tuple.

```
subjects = {1: 'agriculture', 2: 'history', 3: 'government', 4:
            'geography', 5: 'mathematics'}

item = subjects.popitem()
print(item)
print(subjects)
```

Output:
{1: 'agriculture', 3: 'government', 4: 'geography', 5: 'mathematics'}
(5, 'mathematics')

Looping a dictionary

A dictionary is a sequence of items and just like every other sequence, you can loop through the items in it. Here are a few common ways to loop through a dictionary.

Looping through keys

The simplest way to iterate over a dictionary is to loop through its keys using a for loop:

```
#looping through the keys
subjects = {1: 'agriculture', 2: 'history', 3: 'government', 4:
            'geography'}

for subject in subjects:
    print(subject)
```

Output:
1
2

In the above example, the for loop iterates over the keys of the subjects dictionary, and each key is printed. However, you can also achieve the same result using the get() method as shown below:

```
#looping through the keys
for subject in subjects.keys():
    print(subject)
```

Looping through value

If you want to iterate over the values of the dictionary, you can use the values() method to loop over the values of a dictionary.

```
subjects = {1: 'agriculture', 2: 'history', 3: 'government', 4:
'geography'}
for subject in subjects.values():
    print(subject)
```

Outputs:
agriculture
history
government
geography

Looping through key-value pairs

The items() method allows you to iterate over both keys and values simultaneously.It returns a view object that contains tuples of key-value pairs from the dictionary.

```
#looping through the items
subjects = {1: 'agriculture', 2: 'history', 3: 'government', 4:
          'geography'}

for subject in subjects.items():
    print(subject)
```

Output:
(1, 'agriculture')
(2, 'history')
(3, 'government')
(4, 'geography')

Built-in methods for dictionaries

These are methods that enable you create, alter or manipulate the items in a dictionary.

clear() method

The clear() method removes all the items in a dictionary, producing an empty dictionary.

```
D = {'name':'Andrew', 'age':23, 'married':False, 'colors':['red',
    'green']}

D.clear()
print(D)
```

Outputs:
{}

copy() method

The copy() method is used to create a new dictionary as a copy of another dictionary.

```
D1 = {'name':'Andrew', 'age':23, 'married':False, 'colors':['red',
'green']}
D2 = D1.copy()
print(D2)
```

Outputs:
{'name': 'Andrew', 'age': 23, 'married': False, 'colors': ['red', 'green']}

fromkeys() method

The fromkeys() method enables the creation of a new dictionary based on a sequence of items serving as keys, with an optional provision for default values.

To use this method, you are required to provide two arguments: a sequence, such as a list, tuple, or set, and an optional default value (which is set to None).

```
D = dict.fromkeys(['name', 'age', 'gender'], '-')
print(D)
D = dict.fromkeys(['name', 'age', 'gender'])
print(D)
```

Outputs:
{'name': '-', 'age': '-', 'gender': '-'}
{'name': None, 'age': None, 'gender': None}

> **Pro Tip:**
> *If no argument is provided for default values for the items, the items will have values of None.*

get() method

This method retrieves the value associated with a specified key in a dictionary, provided that the key exists.

```
student = {'age': 21, 'gender': 'male'}
age = student.get('age')
gender = student.get('gender')
print(age)
print(gender)
```

Output:
21
male

items() method

This method returns a dictionary object of the items in a dictionary in keys and values pairs.

```
student = {'age': 21, 'gender': 'male'}
print(student.items())
#output
dict_items([('age', 21), ('gender', 'male')])
```

keys() method

This method returns a dictionary object of the keys in a given dictionary.

```
student = {'age': 21, 'gender': 'male'}
print(student.keys())
#output
dict_keys(['age', 'gender'])
```

values() method

This method returns a dictionary object of values contained in a given dictionary.

```
student = {'age': 21, 'gender': 'male'}
print(student.values())
```

Output:
dict_values([21, 'male'])

pop() method

The pop() method is used to remove items from a dictionary. Unlike in sequences such as lists, sets or tuples, you are required to provide the key as argument in the pop.

It removes the item and returns the value of the item as shown below:

```
D = {'name': 'Kenny', 'age': 21, 'gender': 'male'}
person = D.pop('name')
print(person)
print(D)
age = D.pop('age')
print(age)
print(D)
```

Output:
Kenny
{'age': 21, 'gender': 'male'}
21
{'gender': 'male'}

popitem() method

This behaves like the pop() method, except that it doesn't require an argument. It removes the last item in a dictionary and returns a tuple of the key value pair.

```
D = {'name': 'Kenny', 'age': 21, 'gender': 'male'}
person = D.popitem()
print(person)
print(D)
person = D.popitem()
print(person)
print(D)
```

Output:
('gender', 'male')
{'name': 'Kenny', 'age': 21}
('age', 21)
{'name': 'Kenny'}

setdefault() method

This is used to return the value of a given key or add and assign a key to a value if the key is not in the dictionary.

```
D = {'name': 'Kenny', 'age': 21, 'gender': 'male'}
name = D.setdefault('name')
print(name)

level = D.setdefault('level')
print(level)
print(D)

complexion = D.setdefault('complexion', 'black')
print(complexion)
print(D)
```

Output:
Kenny
None
{'name': 'Kenny', 'age': 21, 'gender': 'male', 'level': None}
black
{'name': 'Kenny', 'age': 21, 'gender': 'male', 'level': None, 'complexion': 'black'}

update() method

This method is used to add the items of dictionary to an already existing dictionary.

```
student = {'name': 'kevin', 'age': 21, 'gender': 'male', 'major':
'engineering'}
level  = {'year':2}
student.update(level)
print(student)
```

Output:
{'name': 'kevin', 'age': 21, 'gender': 'male', 'major': 'engineering', 'year': 2}

enumerate() method

The enumerate() method converts a dictionary into a list, pairing the positional indexes of each item with the keys.

```
D = {'name':'Kenny', 'age':21, 'phone':'0903-843-9234',
     'major':'engineering'}

print(enumerate(D))
print(list(enumerate(D)))

#looping and printing the items
for item in enumerate(D):
    print(item)
```

Outputs:
<enumerate object at 0x11192b780>
[(0, 'name'), (1, 'age'), (2, 'phone'), (3, 'major')]
(0, 'name')
(1, 'age')
(2, 'phone')
(3, 'major')

Comprehension in dictionaries

Dictionary comprehension shares its syntax with list comprehension but with a slight distinction. It starts with a curly braces, instead of the square bracket as obtainable in the list comprehension.

> **Pro Tip:**
> *Unlike the set comprehension that equally starts with a curly brace, key value pair precedes the opening curly braces in the dictionary comprehension.*

```
result = {num:num**2 for num in [1,2,3,4]}
print(result)
```

Output:
{1: 1, 2: 4, 3: 9, 4: 16}

You can also use the zip() function in dictionary comprehension to combine two list into a dictionary of key value pairs.

```
D = {x for x in zip([1,2,3], [4,5,6])}
print(D)
```

Output:
{(2, 5), (1, 4), (3, 6)}

Summary

This chapter began by delving into the concept of dictionaries and how they are used to store and manipulate data in programming. In this chapter, you learnt how to create dictionaries, access and modify their elements, utilize built-in methods and iterate through dictionary items.

Practice Exercises

1. What is a dictionary?
2. Is dictionary a mutable type or not? Explain the reason for your answer.
3. Write a program to concatenate or join two dictionaries together to get a new one.
4. How do you print all the keys in a dictionary?
5. How do you print all the values in a dictionary?
6. Write a program to determine if a given key is in a dictionary
7. Explain how to create a dictionary using tuples.
8. Explain dictionary comprehension with an example.

## Chapter 10

SETS

"Tones sound, and roar and storm about me until I have set them down in notes."

- Ludwig van Beethoven

Just like the lists, a set is a collection of items. However, unlike the list, all the items in a set are unique. So, if you want to create a list that contains only unique items or remove any duplicates from an existing list, sets are the way to go.

Learning outcome

In this chapter, you will learn:
- What sets are and how they differ from lists and dictionaries.
- To perform various set operations, including union, intersection, difference, and symmetric difference.
- To create sets on the fly using a technique known as set comprehensions.

Introduction

A set is a built-in data type in Python that represents an unordered collection of unique elements. It is primarily used for eliminating duplicate entries from a sequence.

Sets support various mathematical operations like union, intersection, difference, and symmetric difference. They are mutable, meaning you can add or remove elements from them.

You create a set by enclosing a sequence of values separated by commas in curly braces.

```
#creating a set
nums = {1,2,3,4,5}
```

Alternatively, you can pass in a sequence of values as an argument to the set() function to create a set.

```
L = [1,2,3,4,5]
nums = set(L)
```

Pro Tip:
It's important to note that when using curly braces to create an empty set, Python interprets it as an empty dictionary, not an empty set.

So, if you want to create an empty set, it's best to use the set() function instead of the curly braces.

```
#creating an empty set
nums = set()
```

Adding items to a set

The add() method allows you to add a single element to the set. If the element is already present, it won't duplicate it.

```
#adding items to a set
nums = set()
nums.add(1)
print(nums)
nums.add(2)
print(nums)
```

Output:
{1}
{1, 2}

Keep in mind that duplicates values are not allowed in sets. So, if you try to add a duplicate item to a set, it will simply be ignored and not added to the set.

```
nums = set()
nums.add(1)
print(nums)
nums.add(2)
print(nums)
nums.add(2)
print(nums)
```

Output:
{1}
{1, 2}
{1, 2}

Removing items from a Set

If you want to remove a specific element from a set, you can use the remove() method. This method requires that you specify the item you want to remove as an argument.

```
#removing items from a set
nums = {1,2,3,4,5}
nums.remove(3)
print(nums)
```

Output:
{1, 2, 4, 5}

> **Pro Tip:**
> *If you try to remove an item that is not in the set, a KeyError will be raised.*

Removing duplicates with sets

You can efficiently remove duplicates from a list by taking advantage of the unique property of sets.

In the example below, the list L contains duplicate items. By converting the list to a set, you automatically eliminate the duplicates.

```
#removing duplicates from a list
L = [1,2,2,5,6,2,5,7,4,3]
result = set(L)
print(list(result))
```

Output:
[1, 2, 3, 4, 5, 6, 7]

Operations on sets

Sets allows you to perform a wide range of operations including union, intersection, difference, and symmetric difference.

Let's explore each of these operations:

Union

The union of two sets refers to the combination of all the unique elements from both sets. When you perform a union operation on sets, the resulting set contains all the elements from both sets, but without any duplicates.

To perform a union operation, you either use the union() method or the pipe operator |.

```
#union
S1 = {1,2,3,4,5}
S2 = {3,4,5,6,7,8}
result = S1.union(S2)
print(result)
```

Output:
{1, 2, 3, 4, 5, 6, 7, 8}

If you are using the pipe operator, then your code will look like this:

```
result = S1 | S2
print(result)
```

Output:
{1, 2, 3, 4, 5, 6, 7, 8}

As you have seen, both the union() method and the | operator offer convenient ways to perform the union operation on sets. So, you can choose the method that suits your coding style and preference.

Intersection

The intersection of two sets is the set of all elements that are common to both sets. You can perform the intersection operation using either the intersection() method or the bitwise and operator &.

The intersection() method takes another set as an argument and returns a new set that contains the common elements found in both sets.

```
#intersection
S1 = {1,2,3,4,5}
S2 = {3,4,5,6,7,8}

result = S1.intersection(S2)
print(result)
```

Output:
{3, 4, 5}

Alternatively, you can use the bitwise and operator & to perform the intersection operation between sets.

```
result = S1 & S2
print(result)
```

Output:
{3, 4, 5}

Difference

The difference between two sets is the set of all elements in a given set that are not in the other set. You can perform the difference operation using either the difference() method or the minus - operator.

The difference() method takes another set as an argument and returns a new set that contains the elements present in the original set but not in the other set.

```
#difference
S1 = {1,2,3,4,5}
```

```
S2 = {3,4,5,6,7,8}
result = S1.difference(S2)
print(result)
#using the minus operator
result = S1 - S2
print(result)
```

Output:
{1, 2}
{1, 2}

In the above example, S1.difference(S2) calculates the difference between S1 and S2, resulting in a new set that contains the elements {1, 2} which are present in S1 but not in S2.

However, you should know that S1.difference(S2) or S1 - S2 is different from S2.difference(S1) or S2 - S1.

Take a look at this:

```
result = S2.difference(S1)
print(result)
#alternatively
result = S2 - S1
print(result)
```

Outputs:
{8, 6, 7}
{8, 6, 7}

Symmetric Difference

The symmetric difference between two sets is the set of all elements that are in either of the sets, but not in both. You can use the symmetric_difference() method or the caret operator ^ operator to perform a symmetric difference operation between sets.

```
#symmetric difference
S1 = {1,2,3,4,5}
S2 = {3,4,5,6,7,8}
```

```
result = S1.symmetric_difference(S2)
print(result)

#alternatively
result = S1 ^ S2
print(result)
```

Output:
{1, 2, 6, 7, 8}
{1, 2, 6, 7, 8}

Set Comprehension

Sets support comprehensions just like lists. In set comprehension, curly braces is used instead of square brackets.

```
S = {num for num in range(5)}
print(S)
```

Output:
{0, 1, 2, 3, 4}

The interesting thing about set comprehension is that the resulting set from the comprehension is made of only unique items. If you don't want duplicate items or items occurring more than once in a sequence, then set comprehension will give you the outcome.

```
S = {num**2 for num in range(4)}
print(S)
```

Output:
{0, 1, 4, 9}

Cartesian product of sets

A very important application of comprehension in sets is getting the cartesian product of sets. In simple terms, cartesian product of a set is a set comprising all the possible combinations of the items in the set.

Below is an illustration of the cartesian product of two sets.

{a1, a2} x {b1, b2} = {a1, b1}, {a1, b2}, {a2, b1}, {a2, b2}

Now, let's see how to perform cartesian product of sets using set comprehension

```
S1 = {1,2,3}
S2 = {4,5,6}
P = {(x,y) for x in S1 for y in S2}
print(P)
```

Output:
{(2, 4), (3, 4), (1, 5), (1, 4), (2, 6), (3, 6), (1, 6), (2, 5), (3, 5)}

Apart from using set comprehension, you can also use obtain a cartesian product by using simple iteration or the itertools module from the Python standard library.

Cartesian product using simple iteration

Cartesian product can also be achieved using regular iteration as shown below:

```
S1 = {1,2,3}
S2 = {4,5,6}
P = []
for x in S1:
        for y in S2:
        P.append((x,y))

print(P)
```

Output:
[(1, 4), (1, 5), (1, 6), (2, 4), (2, 5), (2, 6), (3, 4), (3, 5), (3, 6)]

from itertools import product

You can make use of the product function in the itertools module to quickly obtain Cartesian product as shown below:

```
from itertools import product
S1 = {1,2,3}
S2 = {4,5,6}
P = product(S1, S2)
print(set(P))
```

Output:
{(2, 4), (3, 4), (1, 5), (1, 4), (2, 6), (3, 6), (1, 6), (2, 5), (3, 5)}

Frozen sets

Frozen set is special kind of sets in python. Unlike the regular set that is mutable, frozen sets are immutable.

To create a frozen set, the frozenset () method is used as shown below:

```
numbers = (1,2,3)
colors = {'red', 'blue', 'green', 'gray'}
fruits = ['apple', 'grape', 'orange']
frozen_numbers = frozenset(numbers)
frozen_colors = frozenset(colors)
frozen_fruits = frozenset(fruits)
print(frozen_numbers)
print(frozen_colors)
print(frozen_fruits)
```

Output:
frozenset({1, 2, 3})
frozenset({'blue', 'red', 'green', 'gray'})
frozenset({'orange', 'grape', 'apple'})

Also, you can easily convert a frozenset to a list or tuple using functions like list or tuple as shown below:

```
print(list(frozen_numbers))
print(tuple(frozen_numbers))
```

Output:
[1, 2, 3]
(1, 2, 3)

Since, frozensets are immutable, operations like discard or update are not allowed, else you will get an error.

```
F = frozenset({1,2,3})
F.discard(1)
```

Output:
AttributeError: 'frozenset' object has no attribute 'discard'

Summary

In this chapter, you learnt concept of sets and how they are used to store and manipulate unique elements in programming. Sets are versatile data structures that offer a distinct set of operations compared to lists and dictionaries. You performed different kinds of set operations including union, intersection, difference, and symmetric difference. Also, you learnt how to create sets on the fly using set comprehensions.

Practice Exercises

1. Write a program that creates a set.
2. Write a program that adds and removes items from a set.
3. Write a program to check if a set is a subset of another set.
4. Write a program to check if two sets contain at least one item in common.
5. Write a program to find elements in a set that is not in another set.
6. How will you remove the duplicate elements from the list?
7. Write a program that converts a set to a dictionary.
8. Write a program to find the size of a set.
9. What is the difference between a set and a list?
10. What is the relationship between a set and a dictionary?
11. Write a program to find the intersection of two lists without using the set or & operator.
12. What is Frozen Set in Python?

## Chapter 11

FUNCTIONS

"The function of the artist is to invent, not to chronicle."
- Oscar Wilde

In a toolbox, every tool is designed with a specific function in mind. Trying to use a tool for a different purpose than intended will simply not yield the desired results. Imagine trying to use a screwdriver to do the job of a hammer! You'll face a lot of difficulty, right? This is because screwdriver just isn't designed for pounding nails. It's meant for turning screws. But what if you try to use the screwdriver to loosen a screw, but you use it in the wrong way? You still won't succeed, and even if you succeed it would not give you the desired outcome. In Python, functions play a similar role to tools in a toolbox. They are defined to perform specific tasks, just like each tool has its own purpose. When you call a function, it executes a set of instructions designed for a particular job.

Learning outcome

In this chapter, you will learn:
- To define and call functions.
- To differentiate between a parameter and an argument.
- Functions with positional, keyword and variable number of arguments.
- To write recursive functions.
- To write lambda or anonymous functions.
- To write generator functions.

Introduction

Functions are a fundamental concept in programming that allow you to break down a complex program into smaller and more manageable pieces.

A function is a group or chunks of codes that perform a given action. It allows you to define a block of code that can be executed multiple times throughout your program.

Instead of duplicating the same code in different places, you can define a function once and call it whenever needed, therefore promoting code reusability.

Each function performs a specific task or operation, making the overall program more organized, easier to understand, and maintainable.

There are two types of functions in python and they include the built-in functions and the user-defined functions. Built-in are predefined functions that comes with the standard python library such as the input(), range() and print() functions. User-defined functions also known as custom functions are created by programmers to serve a given purpose.

Creating a Function

A function is a block of code defined with a name. It can take arguments and return values. You can define a function using the def keyword. This is followed by the name you choose for your function and the necessary parameters enclosed in parentheses.

```
def greet():
    print('hello')
```

The above example is a simple function with the name greet. Inside the function is a print statement that displays "hello".

Once you've defined a function, the next step is to put it to work and make it actually do something.

> **Pro Tip:**
> *A function on its own is just a defined set of actions or operations. It doesn't actively do anything until you call or invoke it.*

Calling a Function

To call a function, you simply provide the name of the function, and then you include a pair of parentheses right after it.

```
#calling function
greet()
```

Output:
hello

When you make the function call, the code inside the function block is executed, and the output "hello" is displayed.

Creating a function with parameters

In the above example, the greet() function was defined without parameters. However, it is common for functions to be defined with one or multiple parameters. This functionality allows you to provide values or information to the function when you call it.

A function parameter is a variable that is specified in the definition of a function. It serves as a placeholder for the values that will be passed into the function when it is called.

Upon calling the function, you provide the actual values or variables as arguments to match the parameters specified in the function's definition.

These arguments are then assigned to the parameters, and the function can use them to perform calculations, manipulate data, or produce a result.

Take a look at this example:

```
#creating a function with parameters
def greet(name):
    print('Hello' + ' ' + name + '!')
```

To call this function, you have to provide the name of the function including the argument(s) as shown below:

```
#calling a function with parameters
greet('Bob')
```

Output:
Hello Bob!

Returning values

When you create a function, you're basically providing a set of instructions to be performed whenever the function is called.

In addition to performing tasks, functions can also be created to return specific values. By using the "return" statement within a function, you can specify the value or values to be sent back whenever the function is called.

When a return statement is encountered in a function, it immediately terminates the function's execution and returns the specified value(s) to the caller.

This means that a function can calculate something or perform some task and then send the result back to you.

> **Pro Tip:**
> *It is important to note that every function returns something and in a situation where a function does not have a return statement, it automatically returns the value None.*

To return a value from a function, you use the return keyword followed by the value to return.

```python
#return statement
def greet(name):
    result = 'Hello' + ' ' + name + '!'
    return result
message = greeting('Bob')
print(message)
```

In the above example, the return statement is used to send back the value stored in the variable "result". By assigning the greet() function to the variable "message", the value returned by the function is stored in "message".

Positional and keyword arguments

There are two ways to provide arguments to a function during a function call, and they include:

1. Positional arguments
2. Keyword arguments

The concept of positional arguments in a function refers to the order in which you provide values or variables when calling that function. When you call a function and provide values without specifying the parameter names, those values are assigned to the parameters in the order they appear in the function's definition.

```
#positional arguments
def add(a, b):
    result = a + b
    return result

result = add(10, 5)
print(result)
```

Output:
15

On the contrary, keyword arguments involves specifying the parameter name along with the corresponding value during the function call. This approach allows you the flexibility to supply values to the function in any desired order, provided that you accurately align them with the correct parameter names.

```
#keyword arguments
def add(a, b):
    result = a + b
    return result

result = add(b=2, a=7)
print(result)
```

Output:
9

In the above example, the add function is defined with two arguments: 'a' and 'b'. Unlike positional arguments, where the arguments are provided in the order defined in the function, here the second argument 'b' is supplied first, followed by the first argument 'a'.

Also, Python allows you to mix positional and keyword arguments in a function call. This way, you can provide values for some parameters based on their position while explicitly specifying values for other parameters using their names.

Pro Tip:
If you are to mix the positional and keyword arguments in a function call, you should provide positional arguments before keyword arguments.

```
def add(a, b, c):
    result = a + b + c
    return result

result = add(1, c=3, b=5)
print(result)
```

Output:
9

Functions with default parameters

When defining a function, you can assign default values to some or all of its parameters. These default values act as fallbacks, allowing the function to be called without explicitly providing values for those parameters. If no value is supplied during the function call, the default value is used.

This is particularly useful when you want to make a parameter optional, providing a fallback value in case the caller does not explicitly pass a value for that parameter.

To define a default parameter, you simply assign a value to the parameter in the function definition as shown in the example below:

```
#default parameters
def add(a=5, b=4):
    result = a + b
    return result

#providing arguments
result = add(1,2)
print(result)
```

Output:
3

```
#without providing arguments
result = add()
```

```
print(result)
```

Output:

9

Functions with variable number of arguments

There are situations where a function needs to handle an unspecified number of arguments. These types of arguments are termed "variable-length arguments" because their quantity can vary.

This is especially useful when you are uncertain about the exact number of arguments that will be supplied to the function.To handle such situations in Python, you can define your function using the *args and **kwargs.

*args

The *args is a special syntax that allows a function to accept a variable number of positional arguments. It allows you to pass multiple arguments to the function without explicitly defining each argument.

When you define a parameter with *args syntax, it collects any number of positional arguments into a tuple.

```
def func(*args):
    for arg in args:
        print(arg)
func('orange', 'purple', 'brown', 'red')
```

Outputs:

orange
purple
brown
red

**kwargs

The *kwargs is a special syntax that allows a function to accept a variable number of keyword arguments. It allows you to pass multiple keyword arguments to the function without explicitly defining each argument.

When you define a parameter with **kwargs syntax, it collects any number of keyword arguments into a dictionary.

```
#**kwargs
def func(**kwargs):
    for key in kwargs:
        print(key, '=>', kwargs[key])
func(name='Eva', sex='male', age=9, nationality='France')
```

Output:
name => Eva
sex => male
age => 9
nationality => France

Recursive functions

A recursive function is a function that calls itself during its execution. Recursive functions break down a problem into smaller subproblems and solve each subproblem by applying the same approach.

To understand recursion, let's explore its application in determining the factorial of a number.

```
def factorial(num):
    if num == 1:
        return 1
    else:
        return num * factorial(num-1)


number = 5
result = factorial(number)
print(result)
```

The above example uses recursion to calculate the factorial of a given number. The function multiplies the number by the factorial of its decrement until it reaches the base case (num equals 1).

Anonymous/Lambda functions

A lambda function is a simple function that can be defined without a name.. It is also known as an anonymous function because it doesn't require the use of the def keyword to create a function with a name.

Lambda functions are commonly used when a simple, one-line function is needed for a specific operation or when a function is required as an argument to another function.

A lambda function is created using the keyword "lambda".

```
#lambda functions
add = lambda a, b: a + b
result = add(3,5)
print(result)
```

Output:
8

In the above example, the lambda keyword is used to create an anonymous function and a, b are the arguments it takes. The expression a + b is the operation it performs, which is simply adding the two numbers. This is like saying "create a function called add that adds two numbers a and b together".

This function is then invoked using the name "add" followed the arguments 3 and 5 inside a parentheses.

Generator functions

Generator functions are a special type of functions that return iterator objects. Unlike regular functions where the return statement signifies the end of execution, in generator functions, the yield statement is employed to pause temporarily, preserving the current state.

When yield is used, the function provides a value and then pauses until the next invocation. Upon subsequent calls to the function, it resumes from where it left off, maintaining its prior state.

This way, you can gradually obtain values from the function on successive calls, instead of getting everything at once.

> **Pro Tip:**
> *Generator functions are useful in scenarios where you need to process large amounts of data.*

Creating Generators

To define a generator function, you use the def keyword followed by the name and the parameters.

However, instead of using the return statement to return a value, you use the yield statement to produce a value.

```
#generator function
def num_gen(n):
    for i in range(n):
        yield i
```

When a generator function is called, it doesn't execute the body of the function immediately. Instead, it returns a generator object that can be iterated over.

If you want to access all the numbers at a time, you can iterate over the generator using a for loop as shown below:

```
gen = num_gen(5)
for num in gen:
    print(num)
```

Output:

0

1

2

3

4

Also, you can use the iter() and next() functions to retrieve values from generator functions sequentially. The process involves creating an iterator using iter() and then retrieving values one at a time with next().

```
gen = num_gen(3)
iter1 = iter(gen)
print(next(iter1))
print(next(iter1))
```

Output:

0

1

2

Generating even numbers using a generator function

Now, let's create a simple generator function that produces even numbers. The key idea is to use loops to generate numbers and yield only the even ones.

```
#generating even numbers
def even_numbers(n):
    i = 0
    while i < n:
        yield i
        i += 2

gen = even_numbers(10)
for num in gen:
    print(num)
```

Output:

0

2

4
6
8

Generator Expressions

Generator expressions allows you to create generators without explicitly defining functions. The syntax is similar to that of list comprehension except that the expression is wrapped inside a parenthesis instead of the square bracket.

Consider the following example:

```
squares = (x ** 2 for x in range(1, 5))
for square in squares:
    print(square)
```

Here, the generator expression is used to create a generator object square. If you iterate over this object, you will get the following output.

1
4
9
16

Now, let look at another example but this time, we will be generating odd numbers using a generator expression.

```
#Generating odd numbers using a generator expression
numbers = [1, 2, 3, 4, 5, 6, 7, 8, 9, 10]
odd_nums = (num for num in numbers if num % 2 != 0)
for num in odd_nums:
    print(num)
```

Output:
1
3
5
7

9

Summary

This chapter began by explaining the concept of functions and how they are used to organize and reuse code in programming. You learnt how to define and call functions. You learnt the difference between parameters and arguments and how to work with various types of function arguments. Also, you learnt how to write recursive functions, lambda or anonymous functions and generator functions.

Practice Exercises

1. Define a function that accepts two numbers and returns the maximum.
2. What do you mean by function arguments and parameters?
3. What is a namespace in Python?
4. What is recursion?
5. Define a function that can accept variable number of arguments and returns the sum and average.
6. Define a function that counts the vowels and consonants in a word.
7. Define a function that accepts radius and returns the area of a circle.
8. What is the difference between lambda functions and regular functions?
9. When is it appropriate to use a lambda function?
10. What are generators?
11. What are the benefits of using generators in Python?
12. What is the difference between generators and generator expressions?
13. What is the yield keyword used for in Python?
14. How do you iterate over a generator in Python?
15. Write a program that generates a Fibonacci series.
16. Using iterative technique, write a program that calculates the factorial of a number.

## Chapter 12

MODULES

"Really, the only thing that makes sense is to strive for greater collective enlightenment."
- Elon Musk

Instead of dealing with one long, complex piece of code, you can break it down into smaller, independent bits. When you break down the code into smaller components, it makes it more manageable and easier to work with. Because they are independent, you can improve or work on any of them without having to worry about the rest. These independent pieces of code are called modules.

Learning outcome

In this chapter, you will learn:
- To use modules to organize your code into separate reusable files.
- The different techniques for importing modules.
- The vast collection of Python Standard Library and how to use them.
- To create package directories and define package-level functionalities.

Introduction

In Python, a module is simply a file containing Python expressions and statements, allowing you to organize your code into reusable components.

Instead of writing the same code over and over again, you may decide to create a module and use it over and over in different programs. This not only saves you time but also makes the code easier to maintain and debug.

Python comes with a standard library comprising modules files with different functions and classes that allow you to perform different kinds of operations.

Creating a module

Modules facilitate code organization, reusability, and collaboration. To create a Python module file, you can follow these steps:

1. Open a text editor or an integrated development environment (IDE).
2. Create a new file and save it with a .py extension.

3. Write Python statements inside the file, in form of functions, classes, variables, and other valid Python constructs.
4. Save the file after you have finished writing the code for your module.

Once you have completed these steps, you have created a Python module. You can then use this module by importing it in other Python scripts or programs.

Importing a module

To access or use the definitions contained in a module from another program, you have to import the module. This is done using the "import" keyword followed by the name of the module you want to import.

```
import mod
```

By importing a module, you gain access to its definitions within your program.

Python provides several ways to import and use modules in your programs. Here are some of the most common ways:

- Importing the entire module
- Importing specific names
- Importing with an alias
- Importing all definitions

Importing the entire module

You can import the entire module using the import keyword followed by the module name.

```
import mod
```

This method imports the whole module and makes all its definitions and statements available in the current program.

Importing specific names

If you don't want to import all the definitions and statements in a module, you can selectively select the ones you want to use by using the from keyword followed by the module name, then specifying the desired definitions.

```
from mod import multiply
from mod import divide
```

The above example uses the from keyword to import specific names from the module and makes them available in the current program. This can be useful if you only need a few functions or variables from a large module.

Importing with an alias

Aliases provide a convenient way to rename modules, classes, or functions, making them easier to reference in your code. They are useful in situations where module names are lengthy and need to be shortened, or when module names or their internal names conflict with names already present in your program, requiring the use of alternative names.

By using the "as" keyword, you have the ability to assign an alias, which is a different or shorter name, serving as a replacement for the original module or name within your code.

```
#importing with an alias
import mod as md
from mod import multiplication as mp
```

Importing all definitions

To import all the definitions from a module without explicitly specifying each one, you can use the from keyword followed by the module name, the import keyword and the asterix symbol(*).

```
from mod import *
```

Reloading modules

Importing modules is an expensive process and you are not allowed to import modules more than once in Python. However, there are times when it becomes extremely necessary to do so. In such cases, you can make use of the reload() function of the importlib module.

```
import greeting
import importlib
#reload module greeting
importlib.reload(greeting)
```

Standard Library Module

Python comes with a large collection of modules known as the standard library. Modules like math, os, datetime, unittest and so on are part of the python's standard library.

You can import these modules the same way that you import the ones that you created.

```
import maths
#find the square root of a number
num = math.sqrt(4)
print(num)
```

Output:
2.0

Dir() Function

The dir() function is used to determine the names that are defined in a module. If you are unsure of the namespaces or attributes of a module, you can quickly check this out using this function.

```
import math
dir(math)
```

Module search path

This has to do with the places where python searches for a module file when it encounters an import statement.

When you import a module in a script or another module. Python searches for the module file in the current working directory.

If the module is not there, it then proceeds to search for it in the directories available in the python path and then in the directories for the standard library.

If no such module exists, then it will raise an exception – ModuleNotFoundError.

Packages

A package is simply a directory containing modules. While modules are used for organizing code components into files, packages are used for organizing module files into directories.

To create a python package, all that is required is to create a directory and put module file(s) into it.

In the past, a directory is required to contain a python file with the name __init__.py to be considered a python module, but it's no longer compulsory.

Package import

Indeed, packages make it easy to organize your modules. Now, let's look at how you can import the modules or access the attributes of modules contained in packages.

There are two ways of performing package imports and they include:

- Relative import
- Absolute import

Relative Import

In relative imports, you specify the module you want to import by providing its path relative to the current working directory.

Let's say that you have a directory named pkg that contains another directory named pkg1. The directory pkg1 contains a module file with the name mod1.py.

Imagine you are to create a new module named mod in the pkg directory and want to import the module mod1, which is in the pkg directory, you can easily do so using the relative import.

```
#relative import
from pkg1 import mod1
```

Since the package – pkg1 and the module mod are at the same level in the directory, you can simply refer to the package with just the name.

Now, let's say that pkg1 contains another module named mod2.py and you want to import mod1 in mod2. Since mod1 and mod2 are in the same package, they are considered siblings. Hence, you can use a leading dot (.) to indicate a package import as shown below:

```
#To import mod1 in mod2
from . import mod1
```

The . specifies that the module named mod1 is in the same package as the mod2.

Now, let's say the parent directory pkg contains another package named pkg2, which contains a module – mod3.

This means that packages – pkg1 and pkg2 are siblings. To import mod3 into mod1, you will have to use two leading dots (..).

```
#import mod3 in mod1
from .. import mod3
```

Absolute Import

An absolute path contains the full path of the package being imported starting from the root directory to the module that you are interested in.

Let's say that you want to import the module mod which is contained in the package pkg from the mod1 module.

```
#Absolute import
from pkg import mod
```

Summary

This chapter began by explaining the concept of modules and packages, which are essential for organizing and reusing code in Python. You learned how to create your own modules. You learnt how to use modules by importing them into your programs. Also, you learnt how to leverage the vast collection of Python standard library modules. Finally, you learnt how create package directories to define package-level functionalities.

Practice Exercises

1. What is the essence of creating modules?
2. What are the all ways, by which you can import a module in Python?
3. How can I import the all the functions and variable from a module?
4. What is the difference between a module and a package?
5. What is the difference between import and from module import statements?
6. What are the most common built-in modules in Python?
7. Write a program that converts currencies. You can use Dollar, Pounds and Euro.

## Chapter 13

FILES

"I have files, I have computer files and, you know, files on paper. But most of it is really in my head. So God help me if anything ever happens to my head!"

- George R. R. Martin

A file serves as a container where we can store our documents. And just like in the physical world, when we have a large number of documents, we can get more files to accommodate them. Sometimes, we even group related documents together and place them in a single file. We can label the files to give them meaningful names, making it simpler to locate specific information later on. So, whenever we want to find certain information, we start by looking for the file that contains it, then locate the specific document within that file, and finally, retrieve the desired information. It's interesting how this concept translates to computers as well. Whether we're creating documents, storing photos, or working on projects, files play a central role in our computer-related tasks.

Learning outcomes

In this chapter, you will learn:
- To create, read, write and update files.
- To work with binary data.
- To create, rename, and delete file and directories.

Introduction

In practically every computer-related task, it is highly likely that you will need to interact with files in some form or another. Working with files is a common and fundamental aspect of computing, whether it involves reading, writing, modifying, or managing data stored in files.

A lot of times, we save information in files with the intention of utilizing it later or to facilitate convenient access and sharing whenever needed.

Interestingly, Python provides a convenient way to create, modify, and delete any part of a file. Whatever it is that you want to do, whether it checking the number of words in a file or extracting certain information from a spreadsheet, you can easily do so using Python.

Now, let's see how you can create and manipulate files in Python.

open() function

The open() function is essentially used in almost every operation involving files and file management in Python. It is used to create a file object that allows you to read, write or modify the contents of any given file.

To use this function, you are required to provide arguments including the file name, file path, and access mode, and the syntax is as follows:

file = open(path+filename, mode)

The path is the location of the file you want to access or manipulate, while the mode specifies the kind of operations to be performed on the file.

If you wish to read the contents of an existing file, you can utilize the 'r' mode, which indicates that the access is limited to read-only.

Take a look at the example below:

```
file = open('data.txt', 'r')
```

Here, the open() method is used to the file 'data.txt'. By passing the file name as the first argument ('data.txt') and specifying the 'r' mode as the second argument, the file is opened in read-only mode.

It's important to note that if you don't specify the mode explicitly, the default mode is 'r' (read-only). So, in this case, even if the mode is not specified, the file will still be opened in read-only mode.

So, you can as well write:

```
file  = open('data.txt')
```

Access modes

The access mode is used to specify the permissions and operations that can be performed on a file when it is opened using the "open()" function. By specifying the appropriate access mode, you can control how the file is accessed and manipulated within your program.

Below are the commonly used access modes for accessing or manipulating files in Python.

- **Read-only mode ('r')** - reading the contents of a file but does not allow modifications or writing to the file.
- **Write mode ('w')** - creating a new file andoverwriting an already existing file.
- **Append mode ('a')** - adding new data to the end of the file without overwriting the existing contents.
- **Read-only binary mode ('rb')** - reading the contents of the file as binary data.
- **Write binary mode ('wb')** - writing binary data to the file and overwriting an alreading existing contents.

Reading files

To access the content of an existing file, you can utilize the read-only mode to read or fetch its content.

```
#reading file contents
file = open('data.txt', 'r')
```

The above code creates a file object or a connection to the file. With file object at your disposal, you can proceed to read the entire contents of the file.

Now, let's examine the methods provided by Python that you can use to read or retrieve the content stored within a file.

read() method

The read() method allows you to retrieve the entire content of the file as a single string. With this method, you can retrieve the entire content of a file in one go.

```
#read method
content = file.read()
print(content)
```

Output:
Line 1
Line 2
Line 3

readlines() method

This method involves reading the complete contents of the file and generating a list. By using the readlines() method, the file is read line by line, and each line is stored as an item in a list.

```
#readlines method
content = file.readlines()
print(content)
```

Output:
['Line 1', 'Line 2', 'Line 3']

readline() method

This method fetches the lines in a file one at a time. It is particularly useful if you want to loop through the contents of a file and print or perform a specific action for each loop interval.

```
#readline method
content = file.readline()
for line in content:
    print(line)
```

Output:
Line 1
Line 2
Line 3

Writing to a file

To write to a file, you begin by creating a file object with the write access mode ('w'). This allows you to create a new file or overwrite the contents of an existing file.

```
#writing to a file
file = open('data.txt', 'w')
```

By using the 'w' mode, you indicate that you want to open the file for writing. If the file already exists, opening it in write mode will truncate its contents, meaning that any existing data in the file will be erased. If the file doesn't exist, a new fil e with the specified name will be created.

After opening the file in write mode, you can then use the write() method to write content into the file.

```
for num in range(1,6):
    content = f'line {num}\n'
    file.write(content)
```

In the above example, the for loop is used together with the range function to write the texts 'line 1' to 'line 5' in the file.

Appending to a file

When writing to a file, you have the option to insert new content without overwriting the existing content by using the append method.

When you open a file in append mode ('a'), any data you write to the file will be added at the end, thereby preserving the existing content. If the file doesn't exist, a new file will be created.

```
#appending to a file
file = open('data.txt', 'a')
content = 'line 6'
file.write(content)
```

Closing a file

It is good practice to close files when you are done working with them. By closing files when you're done with them, you release valuable system resources and ensure that your data is securely stored and protected.

You can close a file by calling the close() method on the file object.

```
#closing the file
file.close()
```

Alternatively, you have the option to wrap your file operations within a with statement, which automatically takes care of closing the file when you exit the code block.

```
#file operations using with statement
with open('data.txt', 'w') as file:
    content = 'hello there!'
    file.write(content)
```

This simplifies the process and ensures that the file is closed properly without the need for manual intervention.

Working with binary data

Fundamentally, a computer stores data in bytes. The simplest unit of data storage in computer is 1 byte. So, whether you are working with strings, integer, list and so on, it's eventually stored as bytes in a computer.

Interestingly, bytes are not human readable. They are essentially sequences of 1s and zeros. A byte is prefixed with "b " in Python.

```
b'hello'
b'100'

print(type(b'hello'))
```

Output:
<class 'bytes'>

In binary data, each character is represented by a sequence of bits based on the character encoding used. You can use the ord() method in Python to retrieve the Unicode code point of a character.

```
data = b'hello'
for num in data:
     print(num)
```

Output:
104
101
108
108
111

```
print(ord('h'))
print(ord('e'))
print(ord('l'))
print(ord('o'))
```

Outputs:
104
101
108
111

Pro Tip:
The Unicode code refers to the unique numerical value assigned to each character in the Unicode standard. Unicode is a standardized character encoding system that assigns a unique number (code point) to every character across different writing systems and languages.

Decode Function
To convert a byte to a string, the decode() function is used.

```
data = b'hello'
print(data.decode())
```

Output:
hello

You can also use the str() function to do the same, passing in the encoding format.

```
data = b'hello'
print(str(data, encoding='utf-8'))
```

Output:
hello

Bytearrays

A bytearray is a mutable sequence of integers, each representing a byte of data. Unlike strings, which are immutable, bytearrays allow for in-place modifications.

```
data = b'hello'
b_data = bytearray(data)
print(b_data)
```

Output:
bytearray(b'hello')

Converting string to bytearray

Bytearrays offer a mutable sequence of bytes that is well-suited for handling raw binary data efficiently. You can use the bytearray() constructor to create a bytearray from a string, specifying the desired encoding.

```
b_data = bytearray('hello', 'utf-8')
print(b_data)
```

Output:
bytearray(b'hello')

In contrast, you can use the decode() function to convert a given bytearray to string.

```
data = bytearray('hello', 'utf-8').decode()
print(data)
```

Output:
hello

Writing binary data to file

```
data = b'hello'
file = open('data.txt', 'wb')
file.write(data)
file.close()
file = open('data.txt', 'rb')
output = file.read()
print(output)
```

Output:
b'hello'

Working with CSV Files

CSV, an acronym for comma-separated values, is a text-based file format where data items are separated by commas. While commas are commonly used as delimiters in CSV files, it's important to note that occasionally other characters, including tabs, may also serve as delimiters.

Python's csv module provides a convenient and efficient way to work with CSV files. It offers functions for both reading from and writing to CSV files.

Reading CSV files

To read data from a CSV file, you can use the csv.reader object to iterate through rows and access individual values.

```
import csv
file = open('data.csv', 'r')
reader = csv.reader(file)
for row in reader:
        print(row)
```

Output:
['1', '2', '3', '4', '5']

```
['6', '7', '8', '9', '10']
['11', '12', '13', '14', '15']
```

In the case where the CSV has tab delimiter, you can read the CSV file as thus:

```
reader = csv.reader(file, delimiter=' \t')
```

Writing CSV files

The csv module provides a range of methods for writing data to CSV files. One of the easiest methods involves using the csv.writer object to write data to a CSV file.

Subsequently, the writerow() or writerows() methods can be used to add content to the CSV file.

```
file = open('data.csv', 'w', newline='')
writer = csv.writer(file)
writer.writerow([1,2,3])
file.close()
```

You might as well write multiple rows at once using the writerows() method, which accepts nested lists.

```
content = [['Fruit 1', 'Fruit 2', 'Fruit 3'], ['Apple', 'Orange',
            'Mango']]

with open('data.csv', 'w', newline='') as file:
    writer = csv.writer(file, delimiter=',')
    writer.writerows(content)
```

DictReader() method

This method involves parsing a CSV file and representing its contents as a dictionary. In contrast to the csv.reader, which provides rows as lists, DictReader presents rows as dictionaries.

```
file = open('data.csv', 'r')
```

```
reader = csv.DictReader(file)
for row in reader:
     print(row)
```

Output:

{'Fruit 1': 'Apple', 'Fruit 2': 'Orange', 'Fruit 3': 'Mango'}
{'Fruit 1': 'Pineapple', 'Fruit 2': 'Pawpaw', 'Fruit 3': 'Grape'}

DictWriter()

When using DictWriter, you can structure your data as dictionaries. The DictWriter allows you to use dictionaries to write data to CSV file, with the keys serving as the header row in the CSV file.

```
labels = ['color1', 'color2']
file = open( 'data.csv', 'w', newline='')
writer = csv.DictWriter(file, fieldnames=labels)
writer.writeheader()

writer.writerow({'color1':'green', 'color2':'purple'})

writer.writerow({'color1':'orange', 'color2':'white'})
writer.writerow({'color1':'violet', 'color2':'red'})

file.close()

file = open('data.csv', 'r', newline='')
reader = csv.DictReader(file)

for row in reader:
     print(row)
```

Output:

{'color1': 'green', 'color2': 'purple'}
{'color1': 'orange', 'color2': 'white'}
{'color1': 'violet', 'color2': 'red'}

Copy files

Whether you're working on data processing or simple file management, Python provides a wide range of tools to handle file operations. Within Python's standard library, the shutil module provides a diverse range of functions for executing file operations and manipulations.

One of the functions provided by the shutil module is copy(), which is specifically designed for copying files. The copy() function allows you to create a copy of a file.

It accepts two arguments; the first one is the source or path file that you want to copy, and the second argument being the destination directory.

```
import shutil
shutil.copy('data.txt', 'newfolder/data1.txt')
```

If you execute this code, the file 'data.txt' will be duplicated and stored as 'data1.txt' in the 'newfolder' directory.

Move files

The move() method from the shutil module allows you to move files from one location to another in your computer.

To use the move() method, you need to provide two arguments. The first argument represents the source file or its path that you wish to move, while the second argument specifies the destination directory where you want to place the file.

```
#move files
shutil.move('data.txt', 'newfolder')
```

If you run this code, the "data.txt" file will be moved from its current location to the "newfolder" directory.

Rename file

If you want to rename a file using Python, you can simply make use of the rename() method in the os module.

Not only can you rename individual files, but you can also perform bulk renaming of multiple files in a directory.

Let's see how to rename a file using the rename() method.

```
#rename a file
import os
os.rename('data.txt', 'data2.txt')
```

When this code is executed, the file "data.txt" will be renamed to "data2.txt" in the same location.

Delete file

You can use the remove() method from the os module to permanently delete a file or directory from the file system.

```
#remove a file
os.remove('data2.txt')
```

If you run this code, the file "data2.txt" will be permanently deleted from the file system. This means that it cannot be recovered from the operating system's trash or recycle bin. Hence, it is important to use this method with caution to avoid unintentional data loss.

Summary

In this chapter, you learnt how to create, read, write, and update files. You learnt how to open files using the built-in open() function and specify the desired file mode. You learned how to write data to files, either by overwriting the existing content or appending to the end of the file. Also, you learnt how to work with binary files and perform various operations on files and directories, such as creating, renaming, and deleting them.

Practice Exercises

1. What is file handling in Python?
2. Explain the different modes of opening a file.
3. How do you read and write to an existing file?
4. Write a program to open a text file so that contents can be added at the end.
5. Write a find and replace function that replaces a given text in a document with another text.
6. Write a one-liner that will count the number of capital letters in a file. Your code should work even if the file is too big to fit in memory.
7. Write a program to read from a file and count the particular word occurrence.
8. What is the difference between binary and text files?
9. Write a program that performs bulk renaming and deleting of files.

## Chapter 14

OOP IN PYTHON

"Everything we call real is made of things that cannot be regarded as real."
- Niels Bohr

If you want to build a house, the first thing you would do is to come up with a building plan. The building plan serves as a blueprint, outlining the structure, layout, and design of the house. With the plan in place, you can proceed with constructing the physical building based on that design. Without the plan, it would be challenging to create a cohesive structure. The plan serves as a guide for the construction process, ensuring that all the necessary elements come together harmoniously. This concept applies to programming as well, specifically in the realm of object-oriented programming.

Learning outcome

In this chapter, you will learn:
- To define and instantiate classes.
- To access class attributes and methods through their objects.
- The differences between instance variables and class variables.
- To use inheritance and composition to create reusable codes.

Introduction

Object-oriented programming is one of the most efficient ways of writing programs. It is an approach to programming where programs are organized into classes and objects.

By following the principles of object-oriented programming, you can write programs that model real-life objects such as cars, buildings, trees, animals, people and even places.

Let's say that you want to build a house. It's inevitable that you would need a building plan.

While the plan itself is not the same as the physical building, it serves as an essential foundation for its construction. Thus, the building plan is the template upon which the physical building is built.

In essence, whether you want to build a house, car, furniture or bridge, you need a plan or blueprint.

In the realm of programming, object-oriented programming provides a structured and organized approach to software development, acting as a foundation or template for building robust and scalable applications.

By leveraging the power of OOP, you can design and implement solutions that model real-world entities, providing a natural and intuitive way to represent and manipulate data within your programs.

Classes and objects in Python

Classes and objects are fundamental concepts in object-oriented programming. While classes provide the template used in creating objects, the object itself refers to only a specific object.

With a building plan, you can construct as many buildings as you wish from it. In the same manner, with a class, you can create as many objects as you wish from it.

Now, let's look at it this way.

Imagine that you want to build an estate comprising several houses. No doubt, building an entire estate at once may be overwhelming.

So, an effective approach would be to break down the project into smaller projects. Instead of building all the houses at a time, you may decide to build one house at a time, until the entire estate is completed.

The same concept is applicable in programming. Instead of tackling a complex project head-on, you can break it down into several smaller units or objects.

A class is created using the keyword class followed by the name of the class and a colon. An indented block of code under this definition serves as the body of the class.

```
#creating a class
class Car:
    #do nothing
    pass
```

You can name your classes whatever you like, as long as you choose valid identifier names. But, it isa good practice to use names that are simple and descriptive, and by conventions, class names are capitalized. This makes it possible for other people to easily figure out what a class does from the name.

> **Pro Tip:**
> *A valid identifier name must begin with a letter or underscore, followed by letters, underscores, or digits. Reserved words are not allowed as identifier names.*

Instantiating a class

Objects are created from classes and the process of creating objects is known as instantiation.When you instantiate a class, you create a unique copy of the class with its own set of instance variables and methods.

To instantiate a class in Python, you use the class name followed by parentheses, which may contain any arguments required by the class's constructor.

The syntax for instantiating a class in Python is as follows:

object_name = ClassName(arguments)

Components of a class

In simple terms, when you define a class, you are specifying the attributes and behaviours that objects created from that class will have. Attributes describe the features or characteristics of an object, providing information that helps describe the object itself.

Behaviours, on the other hand, represent the actions or operations that an object can perform.

For instance, you can describe a car with attributes such as manufacturer, type, model and colour. In terms of behaviours, a car can start, move, stop, horn and so on.

When designing classes, attributes are typically implemented as instance variables, whereas behaviours are implemented as methods.

The example below is a class with the name Car with an attribute self.colour and a method move().

```python
class Car:
    def __init__(self, colour):
        #attribute
        self.colour = colour
    def move(self):
        #method
        print("Moving")
```

Constructors

Constructors are provided in classes to serve as the first block of code(s) to be executed whenever an object is being created from them. They are automatically invoked when an object is created from a class, allowing you to perform any necessary setup or initialization tasks.

In python, a special method with the name __init__ () serves as the constructor.

```python
class Car:
    def __init__(self, colour):
        #assign value to instance variable self.colour
```

```
    self.colour = colour
```

When you create an object from this class, the constructor is automatically called, and the provided arguments are passed to it:

```
car =  Car('black')
print(car.colour)
```

Output:
black

Instance variables

An instance variable is a variable that belongs to a specific instance of a class. Instance variables are defined inside the constructor or the __init__() method and is unique to each object created from the class.

They hold data that is specific to an instance, allowing different instances of the same class to have different values for these variables.

An instance variable is defined by specifying the keyword self, followed by a dot and the name of the variable.

```
class Car:
    def __init__(self, name, manufacturer, colour):
        #define and assign values to instance variables
        self.name = name
        self.manufacturer = manufacturer
        self.colour = colour
```

In the example above, self.name, self.manufacturer and self.colour are instance variables specific to each Car object.

Class variables

Class variables are variables that are defined at the top level of a class. Unlike instance variables that are unique to each instance, class variables have the same value for all objects created from that class.

These variables are defined within the class but outside of any class methods.

```python
class Car:
    #class variable
    quantity = 10
    def __init__(self, name, manufacturer, colour):
        #assign values to instance variables
        self.name = name
        self.manufacturer = manufacturer
        self.colour = colour
```

In the provided example, a class variable called 'quantity' is defined within the class. Every instance of the class has the ability to access and modify this variable.

Now, let's create two instances of the class car and see how it works.

```python
car1 = Car('Camry', 'Toyota', 'Black')
car2 = Car('Accord', 'Honda', 'White')
print(car1.quantity)
print(car2.quantity)
```

Output:
10
10

Methods

A method is a function defined inside of a class. However, unlike normal functions, methods contain a compulsory parameter named self. This parameter is required to positioned before any other parameters in a method's definition.

The self parameter represents the object from which the method is being accessed. Whenever there's a method call, python automatically passes the object as an argument to the self parameter.

Methods are often used to access or modify the attributes defined in a class.

```python
class Car:
    #class variable
    quantity = 10
    def __init__(self, name, manufacturer, colour):
        #assign values to instance variables
        self.name = name
        self.manufacturer = manufacturer
        self.colour = colour
    def __init(self, name, manufacturer, colour):
        #define and assign values to instance variables
        self.name = name
        self.manufacturer = manufacturer
        self.colour = colour
    def start(self):
        #method to start the car
        print('starting')
    def move(self):
        #method to move the car
        print('moving')
    def car_info(self):
        #method to get information about the car
        info = f'Car information: {self.colour} {self.name} by
    {self.manufacturer}'
        print(info)
```

Accessing attributes and methods of a class

To access the attributes and methods of the object, you can simply use the object's name followed by a dot (.) and the name of the desired attribute or method as shown below:

```
#accessing attributes and methods
obj = Car('Sunny', 'Nissan', 'Black')
colour =  obj.colour
print(colour)
obj.car_info()
obj.start()
obj.move()
```

Output:
Car information: Black Sunny by Nissan
Black
starting
moving

Modifying the attributes in a class

You can alter or modify the attributes defined in a class from the instance by changing the values of the instance variables or through an interface or method defined in the class.

```
class Car:
    def __init__(self, name):
        self.name = name

    def rename(self, new_name):
        self.name = new_name

#Accessing the value of an instance variable
obj = Car('Honda')
print(obj.name)
#modifying the instance variable through the instance
obj.name = 'BMW'
print(obj.name)

#modifying the instance variable through an interface
obj.rename('Toyota')
print(obj.name)
```

Output
Honda

BMW
Toyota

> **Pro Tip:**
> *Keep in mind that It is not a good practice to alter an instance variable directly through the instance. The best way to do this is through the use of an interface or a specific method provided for such an operation.*

Encapsulation

The concept of encapsulation in object-oriented programming is simply a way of combining attributes and behaviours as a single unit. The essence is to conceal certain attributes and methods from direct access by other objects.

Objects are not supposed to expose all of their attributes and behaviours. Also, objects should not reveal the internal details of the implementations of their methods. Hence, interfaces are provided as gateways to objects' attributes and methods.

When writing your class, it's best that you provide methods known as interfaces from which attributes of the class can be modified or accessed.

```python
#encapsulation
class Shape:
    def __init__(self, length, width):
        #define and assign values to instance variables
        self.length = length
        self.width =  width

    def change_length(self, new_length):
        #change the value
        if self.length > 0:
            self.length = new_length
        else:
            print('enter value greater than 0')
    def change_width(self, new_width):
        #change the value of self.width
        if new_width > 0:
            self.width = new_width
        else:
            print('enter value greater than 0')
```

```
    def area(self):
        #calculate and return the area of a shape
        result = self.length * self.width
        return result
obj = Shape(2,3)
print(obj.area())

#changing a value directly
obj.length =  -3
print(obj.area())

#changing a value through an interface
obj.change_length(-3)
```

Output:
6
-9
enter value greater than 0

In the above example, it is evident that allowing users to directly modify the instance variables can potentially lead to incorrect or undesirable inputs.

However, if you can hide these variables, the users would have no choice but to use the defined interfaces: change_length() and change_width() to alter the values of the instance variables.

Name Mangling

Python provides loose support for encapsulation as methods and attributes are public by default. However, you make the attributes and methods to something close to private using a concept known as name mangling.

Mangled names are sometimes referred to as private names. They are ways in which python restricts access to the names outside of the class.

This is done using single or double-leading underscores on a name to restrict it from direct modification.

```
#name mangling
class Shape:
    def __init__(self, length, width):
        #define and assign instance variables as private
        self.__length = length
        self.__width =  width

    def change_length(self, new_length):
        #change the value of an instance variable
        if new_length > 0:
            self.__length = new_length
        else:
            print('enter value greater than 0')
    def change_width(self, new_width):
        #change the value of an instance variable
        if new_width > 0:
            self.__width = new_width
        else:
            print('enter value greater than 0')

    def area(self):
        result = self.__length * self.__width
        return result

obj = Shape(3,4)
print(obj.__length)
```

Since the variable __length is defined as a private instance variable __length within the Shape class, it cannot be accessed from the object of Shape with the name __length.

Inheritance

Inheritance is an aspect of object-oriented programming where classes or objects inherit the attributes and methods of other classes. This is particularly useful in situations where certain groups of objects share similar characteristics.

With inheritance, you don't always have to write your classes from the scratch. Instead of creating multiple classes, you can create a simple or generic class that the objects you want to model have in common. Subsequently, you can create specialized classes that inherit the attributes and behaviors from this class.

The class which is inherited by another class is called the parent, super or base class, while the class inheriting from another class is called the child, sub or derived class.

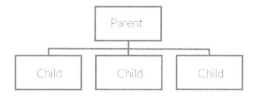

The child class inherits the attributes and behaviours (methods) of the parent class. This means that the child class has access to all the instance variables and methods defined in the parent class.

To indicate that a class is inheriting from another class, you should provide the name of the parent class in parenthesis immediately after the name of the class and before the colon.

```
#parent class
class Animal:
    pass

#child class
class Dog(Animal):
    pass
```

As shown above, Animal is the parent class while Dog is the child class.

Extending and overriding classes

There are basically two things you can do with inheritance and they include:

- Extending
- Overriding

Extending a class means providing additional methods or attributes in the child class while overriding means enhancing or specializing methods in a parent class.

Take a look at this example:

```
class Animal:
    def __init__(self, name, age, gender, colour):
        #define instance variables and assign them with values
        self.name = name
        self.age = age
        self.gender = gender
        self.colour = colour
    def move(self):
        #print moving
        print('moving')
    def make_sound(self):
        #print sound
        print('sound')

    def breathe(self):
        #print breathing
        print('breathing')
```

To extend this class, you have to create a child class that not only inherits from the Animal class but also adds some functionalities that are not present in the parent class.

The example below shows how the child class can extend the parent class by providing additional details that are not available in the parent class.

Let's create a class named Dog that inherits and extends the class Animal.

```
class Dog(Animal):
    def __init__(self, name, age, gender, colour):
        #define the instance variables and assign them with values
        self.name = name
        self.age = age
        self.gender = gender
        self.colour = colour

    #extending the parent class
```

```python
    def run(self):
        #print running
        print('running')

#instantiate the object
dog = Dog('Jacky', 3, 'Male', 'Brown')

#accessing the methods of the parent class
dog.move()
dog.make_sound()
dog.breathe()

#Accessing the run() method defined in the child class
dog.run()
```

Output:
moving
sound
sound
running

From the output of the above code, you can see the Dog class inherited all the attributes of the parent class Animal. It also extended the parent class by defining an additional method run() which is not defined in the parent class.

Overriding a class

Inheritance enables the child class to specialize or enhance methods contained in the parent class. By overriding methods, the child class can customize the behaviour of inherited methods to suit its requirements.

In essence, the child class can reuse the existing method name while providing its own implementation, thereby specializing the method's behaviour.

In Python, you can override a method by defining a method in the child class with the same name as in the parent class.

The example below shows how to override the methods defined in the parent class.

```
class Dog(Animal):
    def __init__(self, name, age, gender, colour):
        #define the instance variables and assign them with values
        self.name = name
        self.age = age
        self.gender = gender
        self.colour = colour

    #overidding the parent class
    def move(self):
        print('run run run...')
    def make_sound(self):
        print('bark bark bark..')
#instantiate the object
dog = Dog('Jacky', 3, 'Male', 'Brown')

#accessing the overridden methods
dog.move()
dog.make_sound()
```

Output:
run run run...
bark bark bark...

Types of inheritance

There are two types of inheritance and they include:

- Single Inheritance
- Multiple inheritance

For a single inheritance, the child class has only one parent class, but for multiple inheritance, the child class has more than one parent class that it is inheriting from.

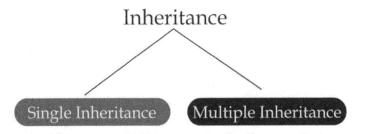

Multiple Inheritance

This is a type of inheritance where a child class has more than one parent class. The child class inherits the attributes and methods of the parent classes.

When accessing any attributes or methods, Python performs a search across all superclasses in accordance with the Method Resolution Order (MRO) until it finds a match.

MRO is also known as diamond patterns defines the sequence in which Python searches for a requested method or attribute. It ensures that the method lookup process follows a consistent and predictable order, preventing ambiguity and conflicts.

The example below is a typical example of multiple inheritance.

```python
class Shape:
    def __init__(self):
        #define and assign value to the instance variable
        self.sides = 1
    def get_name(self, sides):
        #return the name of a shape
        self.sides = sides
        if self.sides == 3:
            return 'Triangle'
        elif self.sides == 4:
            return 'Rectangle'
        elif self.sides == 5:
            return 'Pentagon'
        else:
            return 'shape'


class Colour:
    def __init__(self):
        self.colour = 'colour'

    def get_black(self):
        #return black
        self.colour = 'black'
        return self.colour
```

```python
    def get_blue(self):
        #return blue
        self.colour = 'blue'
        return self.colour

    def get_green(self):
        #return green
        self.colour = 'green'
        return self.colour

class Drawing(Shape, Colour):
    def __init__(self, name):
        self.name = name

#instantiating the object
obj = Drawing('Tree')

#Acessing methods of the Colour class
result = obj.get_black()
print(result)

result = obj.get_green()
print(result)

#Accessing a method in the Shape class
result = obj.get_name(3)
print(result)
```

Output:
black
green
Triangle

In the example above, the Drawing class inherits from the Shape and Colour classes and by virtue of inheritance, it has access to all the attributes and methods of the parent classes.

Composition

Consider an object like the computer, which is made up of many components or objects. A typical computer is made up of objects such as keyboards, speakers, microphones, processors, etc. These objects form the computer system.

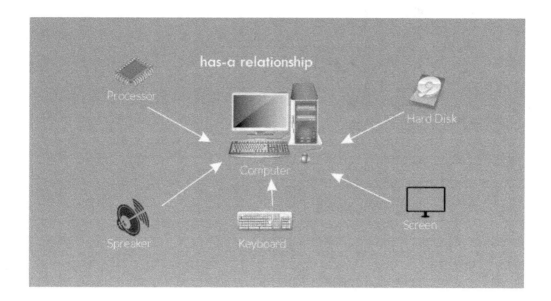

To manufacture a computer, you don't necessarily have to build all these parts on your own. You can simply buy the individual components from different vendors and assemble them together.

You can apply the same principle to model an object such as a computer using the principles of object-oriented programming. By creating classes that represent the different components (objects) and bringing them together, you can assemble these objects into a cohesive unit.

This approach to programming is known as composition. It is a way of writing programs where different objects are combined together to form a single unit. Inside this unit, the individual objects interact with each other in performing tasks.

The relationship between composite object (computer) and the individual objects that makes it up is regarded as has-a relationship. For example, a computer has a keyboard.

To demonstrate this, let's create a class called Computer, consisting of objects such as processors and hard disks.

```
#processor class
class Processor:
    def __init__(self, manufacturer, speed):
        #assign values to the instance variables
        self.manufacturer = manufacturer
```

```python
            self.speed = speed
    def get_manufacturer(self):
        #return the manufacturer
        return self.manufacturer
    def get_speed(self):
        #return the speed
        return self.speed


    def boot(self):
        #boot the processor
        print('booting...')

#harddisk class
class HardDisk:
    def __init__(self, capacity):
        self.capacity = capacity

    def get_capacity(self):
        #return capacity
        return self.capacity


#computer class
class Computer:
    def __init__(self, make, processor, hdd):
        #assign values to the instance variables
        self.make = make
        self.processor = processor
        self.hdd = hdd
    def boot_computer(self):
        #call the boot method of the Processor class
        self.processor.boot()

    def get_hdd_size(self):
        #call the get_capacity method of the HardDisk class
        print('Hard disk size: ' + self.hdd.get_capacity())
    def get_processor_speed(self):
        #call the get_speed method of the processor
        print('Processor speed: ' + self.processor.get_speed())

#instantiating the Processor object
processor = Processor('Intel', '1.8GHz')
```

```
#instantiating the HardDisk object
hdd = HardDisk('500GB')
#instantiating the Computer object
comp = Computer('HP', processor, hdd)
#Accessing the methods of the Computer Class
comp.boot_computer()
comp.get_processor_speed()
comp.get_hdd_size()
```

Output:
booting...
Processor speed: 1.8GHz
Hard disk size: 500GB

In this example, the Computer class employs composition to utilize the Processor and HardDisk classes. Through composition, the Computer object gains access to the attributes and methods of both the Processor and HardDisk objects.

Operator Overloading

In Python, everything is an object, which means that every value or entity in the language is treated as an object. Also, every object has a type, which indicates the specific class or category to which the object belongs to.

The type of an object determines the set of attributes and methods it possesses and defines its behaviour.

For example, if you have two integers and you want to add them together using the "+" operator, you can simply do 3 + 5. Python understands that you're dealing with integers, so it automatically knows how to perform the addition and gives you the result, which in this case is 8.

Similarly, let's say you have two strings and you want to join them. You can use the "+" operator again, like this: "Hello " + "world!". Python recognizes that you're working with strings and intuitively combines them to give you the final result, which in this case is "Hello world!"

However, if you define your own custom types in Python, you may need to specify how the operations should behave for objects of those types. This is where operator overloading comes into play.

Operator overloading allows you to define how operators should work with your custom types. By implementing special methods in your class, you can define the behaviour of operators like +, -, *, ==, etc., for instances of your class.

Consider the example below:

```
#performing additions
num1 = 2
num2 = 3
print(num1+num2)

L1 = [1,2,3]
L2 = [5,6,7]
print(L1+L2)

#performing multiplication
print(num1 * 2)
print(L1*2)
print('hello'*4)
```

Output:
5
[1, 2, 3, 5, 6, 7]
4
[1, 2, 3, 1, 2, 3]
hellohellohellohello

In the above example, the operator + performs addition on numbers but joins or concatenates sequences such as lists and strings. Also, the operator * performs multiplication on numbers but performs repetition on sequences.

So, if you want your classes to support a specific operator, you need to include operator overloading in your class definition.

Operator overloading methods start with two double underscores to keep them distinct from other names in the class. By implementing operator overloading, you can make your custom classes work with various operators, just like the built-in types in Python.

For example, if you want to add two instances of your custom class together using the "+" operator, you need to define the __add__() method within your class. This method should specify how the addition operation should be performed for your class objects.

Here is a list of commonly used operator overloading examples in Python:

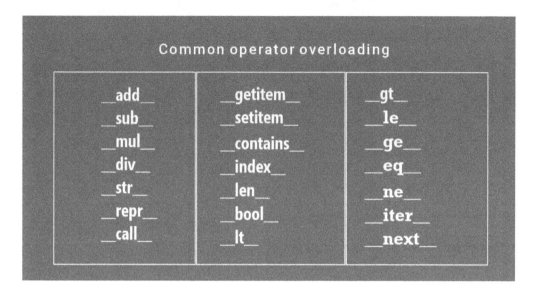

Printing an instance of a class

To print an instance of a custom class, you need to define the __str__() method within the class. This method returns a string representation of the object that you want to display or show when it is printed or converted to a string.

Take a look at this example:

```python
class Car:
    def __init__(self, name):
        #initializing the instance variable
        self.name = name

    def get_name(self):
        #return the instance variable name
        return self.name
```

```
#instantiating the class
obj = Car('Tesla')
print(obj)
```

By printing the instance of this class obj, you will get the following output:

<__main__.Car instance at 0x10b02dcf>

Of course, this is not the outcome that you desire. If you want your object to support printing or to be converted to a string, then you have to implement the __str__() method in your class.

The __str__() method allows you to print or convert an instance of a class into a string format. When you call the print() function or use the str() function on an object, Python looks for the __str__() method within that object's class.

If the method is defined, it is automatically invoked, and the returned string is used for printing or string conversion.

```
class Car:
    def __init__(self, name):
        #initialize the instance variable
        self.name = name

    def get_name(self):
        #return the instance variable
        return self.name

    def __str__(self):
        #result when the instance is printed
        return self.get_name()
#instantiating the class
obj = Car('Tesla')
#print object
print(obj)
```

Output:
Tesla

Overloading arithmetic operators

If you want to perform arithmetic operations on instances of a class, you need to overload the corresponding operators for those operations.

The following example demonstrates a class that overloads arithmetic operators such as +, -, *, and /.

```python
class Numbers:
    def __init__(self, num):
        #define and assign value to the instance variable
        self.num = num**2

    def __add__(self, val):
        #addition
        return self.num + val

    def __sub__(self, val):
        #subtraction
        return self.num - val

    def __mul__(self, val):
        #multiplication
        return self.num * val

    def __truediv__(self, val):
        #division
        return (float(self.num) / val)

#instantiating object
obj = Numbers(3)
num = 2

#addition
result = obj + num
print(result)

#subtraction
result = obj - num
print(result)
```

```
#multiplication
result = obj * num
print(result)

#division
result = obj / num
print(result)
```

Output:

11
7
18
4.5

In the above example, the Numbers class overloads the operators +, -, *, and / using special methods: __add__(), __sub__(), __mul__(), and __truediv__(), respectively.

These methods define how the class instances should behave when the corresponding operators are used on them.

By overloading the operators, you can perform arithmetic operations on instances of Numbers using the familiar syntax of the operators. However, if you perform these operations in a reversed order, you will get an error.

```
#overloading in reverse order.
obj = Numbers(3)
result = 4 + obj
print(result)
```

If you run this code, you will get an error and the reason is that the operand on the left side as the object of the class in which they are defined.

However, there may be cases where the left operand does not support the operation being performed. In such situations, Python provides complementary methods that handle the reverse operation with the right operand as the object of the class, including the __radd__(), __rsub__(), __rmul__() and __rtruediv__() as shown below:

```
class Numbers:
```

```python
    def __init__(self, num):
        #define and assign value to the instance variable
        self.num = num**2

    def __add__(self, val):
        #left addition
        return self.num + val

    def __radd__(self, val):
        #right addition
        return val + self.num

    def __sub__(self, val):
        #left subtraction
        return self.num - val

    def __rsub__(self, val):
        #right subtraction
        return val - self.num

    def __mul__(self, val):
        #left multiplication
        return self.num * val

    def __rmul__(self, val):
        #right multiplication
    return val * self.num

    def __truediv__(self, val):
        #left division
        return (float(self.num) / val)

    def __rtruediv__(self, val):
        #right division
        return (val / float(self.num))

#instantiating object
obj = Numbers(3)
num = 2

#addition
```

```python
result = obj + num
print(result)

result = num + obj
print(result)

#subtraction
result = obj - num
print(result)

result = num - obj
print(result)

#multiplication
result = obj * num
print(result)

result = num * obj
print(result)

#division
result = obj / num
print(result)

result = num / obj
print(result)
```

Now, if you run the code, you will get the following outputs:

11
11
7
-7
18
18
4.5
0.222222222222

Comparing values

Suppose you have a scenario where you need to compare two or more instances of a class using comparison operators (e.g., >, <, >=, <=, ==).

You can accomplish this by overloading the comparison operators, which means defining special methods in your class to handle the comparison operations.

By overloading the comparison operators, you can customize how instances of your class are compared, based on the attributes or criteria that are relevant to your class.

Here's an example to illustrate this concept:

```python
class Square:
    def __init__(self, num):
        self.num = num**2

    def __gt__(self, val):
        #greater than
        result = False
        if self.num > val:
            result = True
        return result

    def __lt__(self, val):
        #less than
        result = False
        if self.num < val:
            result = True
        return result

#instantiating object
obj = Square(3)

print(obj > 5)
print(obj < 5)
```

Output:
True

False

By overloading these comparison methods, you can define the comparison logic for instances of your class. Like the arithmetic operators, comparative operators also have complementary methods including __rlt__(), __rgt__(), __rle__(), __rge__(), __req__() and so on.

Summary

This chapter introduced the concepts of object-oriented programming (OOP) and classes in Python. You learnt how to define and instantiate classes. Also, you learnt how to access class attributes and methods through its objects. Additionally, you learnt how to use inheritance and composition to create reusable code.

Practice Exercises

1. What are the main features of OOP?
2. What are the benefits of OOP?
3. What is the difference between a class and an object?
4. What are the main differences between class variables and instance variables?
5. What are the two types of inheritance in Python?
6. What is a method?
7. Explain how OOP improves code reuse.
8. How does Python implements private and public access?
9. Use an example to explain operator overloading
10. Describe method resolution order for multiple inheritance.
11. How do you check if a class is a child of another class?
12. Write a Python class that converts an integer to roman numeral
13. Write a python class that checks the validity of string parenthesis
14. Write a program to find the three numbers that sum to zero from a set of real numbers.
15. Write a class to implement pow(x,n)
16. Write a program that solves the tower of Hanoi puzzle.
17. Build an interactive command-line quiz.

Chapter 15

EXCEPTIONS

"There are sadistic scientists who hurry to hunt down errors instead of establishing the truth."

- Marie Curie

A lot of times, things do not always go as planned. That's why it's important to have a contingency plan for unexpected situations. Planning for how to respond to unforeseen circumstances can make a significant difference in navigating through life's challenges. Even when we create what seems like a perfect program, unforeseen factors like wrong user inputs or external factors can break it. It can be frustrating when an unexpected error occurs and threatens to crash our program. But how we handle those errors or exceptions really matters to avoid them from causing the program to crash.

Learning outcome

In this chapter, you will learn:
- What exceptions are and how to handle them.
- To use the try-except block to handle different kinds of exceptions.
- To use the else and finally blocks to provide a default action.
- To raise exceptions and create custom exceptions.

Introduction

Exceptions are unexpected events that occur during the execution of a program. These events might disrupt the normal flow of the program and cause it to terminate abruptly if not handled properly.

Hence, it becomes necessary that you handle them correctly to prevent your program from crashing and ensure that it runs smoothly.

Exceptions can occur in a program for various reasons. Even with correct syntax, a program can encounter unforeseen circumstances or encounter data that it cannot handle properly. These unexpected events have the potential to result in exceptions.

Consider a program that attempts to read a file. If the file does not exist or if there are issues with file permissions, an exception may be raised during the execution of the program.

If a program is dependent on the internet to work, and for some reason, the internet service is disrupted, an exception will occur.

When an exception arises, it can lead to the program coming to a halt, and error messages are presented to indicate the reasons behind the sudden interruption. Sometimes, exceptions can be nested or occur in multiple layers which can make it challenging to obtain clear clues about the underlying causes of the errors.

For this reason, it's important to anticipate them in advance and handle them properly and not allow them to disrupt the program flow.

Interestingly, Python provides several mechanisms for handling exceptions, and understanding how to use them can help you write robust and reliable code.

> **Pro Tip:**
> *An error is a general term referring to unexpected issues that can arise during program execution, while an exception is a specific type of error that can be caught and handled through exception handling mechanisms.*

The try-except block

The try-except block is the most commonly used approach for handling exceptions in Python.It provides a structured way to catch and handle exceptions that may occur during the execution of a block of code.

By using try-except blocks, you can catch and handle exceptions gracefully, preventing them from causing the program to crash.

The basic syntax of a try-except block is as follows:

try:
    # Code block where you anticipate an exception
except:
    # Code block to handle the exception

The try block is where you place the code that might raise an exception.If an exception is raised within the try block, the code execution immediately jumps to the except block.

The except block is responsible for handling the exception that occurred in the try block. It contains the code that will be executed to handle the exceptional situation. If no exception is raised, the except block is skipped, and the program continues its normal execution after the try-except block.

To illustrate the concept of exception handling with the try-except block, take a look at this example:

```
#try-except block
try:
    file =  open('data.txt')
    result = file.read()
    print(result)
except:
    print('something went wrong!')
```

In this example, a try-except block is used to handle potential exceptions that may occur while working with a file.

If an exception occurs within the try block, the code execution immediately jumps to the except block to execute the statement print('something went wrong!').

Handling specific exceptions

You can specify the type of exception you want to catch in the except block. This allows you to handle different exceptions differently based on their types.

By specifying the type of exception after the except keyword, you can narrow down the type of exceptions you want to catch and handle.

If the raised exception matches the specified type, the corresponding except block will be executed.

```
#catching a specific exception
try:
    result = input()
    print(result)
except ValueError as e:
    print(e)
```

In this example, the except block specifies ValueError as the exception type to catch. This means that if the user enters an invalid input, a ValueError will be raised.

The except block then catches the ValueError and assigns it to the variable 'e'. Hence, the error message associated with the ValueError can be accessed using the variable 'e'. In this case, it is printed as "Invalid input" along with the specific error message.

Handling multiple exceptions

You can handle multiple exceptions by specifying multiple except blocks or by using a single except block with multiple exception types.

Now, let's see how you can handle multiple exceptions in Python by using multiple except blocks.

```
try:
    result = input()
    print(result)
except ValueError:
    print('Invalid input')
except ZeroDivisionError:
    print('Division by zero not allowed.')
```

This example defined two separate except blocks to handle specific types of exceptions, namely ValueError and ZeroDivisionError.

If a ValueError exception occurs within the try block, the code within the corresponding except ValueError block will be executed. Similarly, if a ZeroDivisionError exception occurs, the code within the except ZeroDivisionError block will be executed.

Else block

When you're writing a program, there might be times when you want it to perform certain actions only if no exceptions are caught. That's where the else block comes into play.

The else block is executed only if no exception is raised within the corresponding try block.

```
try:
    result = 6 * 3
    print(result)
except:
    print('an exception occurred!')
else:
    print("No exceptions occurred!")
```

In this case, no exception occurred and the output is as follows:
18
No exceptions occurred!

Finally block

The finally block is where you put codes that must run regardless of whether an exception is caught or not.

Since codes in the finally block run even when an exception happens, it is a perfect place to perform such garbage collection operations like closing open files to avoid the files from corrupting.

Here's an example demonstrating the use of finally block for closing a file:

```
#finally block
try:
    file = open('data.txt')
    result = file.read()
    print(result)
except:
    print('an exception occurred!')
finally:
    file.close()
```

By using the finally block, you can ensure that vital cleanup operations like closing files, are always executed. Even if exceptions occur, safeguarding your program from potential file corruption or resource leaks.

Raising exceptions

There are situations where it's necessary to deliberately cause an exception at a specific point in your code. This can be really useful because it lets you take control over exceptional situations and handle them in a way that makes sense for your program.

Whether it's dealing with invalid input, detecting errors, or encountering unexpected conditions, you can deliberately trigger an exception and respond to it in a way that ensures your program continues running smoothly.

To do this, you can use the raise keyword.

```
Take a look at this example:
#raise an exception
if num < 0:
        raise ValueError("You cannot use a negative number.")
```

In the above example, the if statement is used to determine whether the variable num is less than zero. If num is less than zero, it raises a ValueError exception with a custom error message, "You cannot use a negative number."

If you put this code inside a try-except block and focus on catching a ValueError, you'll discover that a match will be found.

If you enclose this you enclose this code in a try-block and check for ValueError, and it will turn out positive.

```
try:
    num = -2
    if num < 0:
        raise ValueError("You cannot use a negative number.")
except ValueError as e:
    print(e)
```

Output:
You cannot use a negative number.

User defined exceptions

While Python offers a wide range of built-in exceptions, there are cases where these built-in exceptions may not accurately represent or capture the specific nature of errors encountered in your code.

In such situations, it becomes necessary to create custom exceptions that are tailored to the unique requirements of your program.

By defining your own exceptions, you gain the ability to control over how errors are managed in your code.

You can create a user-defined exception by by defining a new class that inherits from either the built-in Exception class or any of its existing subclasses. This will enable you to inherit essential error handling functionality to your exception class.

Also, creating a user-defined exception gives you the flexibility to add custom attributes and methods to your exception class.

Let's look at an example:

```python
#user-defined exceptions
class CustomError(Exception):
    def __init__(self, message="custom error"):
        self.message = message
```

In the above example, a custom exception class named CustomError is defined, which inherits from the Exception class.

Now, let's raise this exception in a try-except block to see how it works.

```python
#catching user-defined exception
try:
    raise CustomError
except CustomError:
    print('Custom Exception')
```

Output:
Custom Exception

Summary

In this chapter, you learnt what exceptions are and how to handle errors in an application using exception handling. You learnt how to use the try-except block to handle different kinds of exceptions. You also learnt how to use the else and finally blocks for alternatives or to provide a default action. Finally, you learnt how to raise exceptions and even create custom exceptions.

Practice Exercises

1. What is an exception?
2. What is the difference between an exception and errors in Python?
3. How do you handle exceptions in Python?
4. Provide examples of built-in exceptions in Python
5. How do you catch multiple exceptions at once?
6. When will the else part of try-except-else be executed?
7. How would you debug a script that raises an exception?
8. Write a program that demonstrates the importance of raising exceptions.

## Chapter 16

TESTING

"It's easy to make mistakes that only come out much later, after you've already implemented a lot of code. You'll realize Oh I should have used a different type of data structure. Start over from scratch."

- Guido Van Rossum

In factories, products are passed through a process known as quality control to ensure that it meets up with quality requirements or standards. Some companies even have systems in place where products are inspected at every stage of production. This is to ensure that any potential issues or defects are identified and corrected before reaching the final product stage. The same concept applies to programming as well. Just like quality control in factories, testing helps us identify any issues or bugs in the code. It ensures that the program is reliable and performs as intended.

Learning outcome

In this chapter, you will learn:
- The importance of testing in program development.
- To write code that is easily testable.
- To write unit tests using the unittest module.

Introduction

One of the characteristics of a good program is the ability to produce correct results in a consistent manner. Let's say that you have a program that takes a sequence of numbers as input and produces the sum of the numbers as output.

It is expected of it to produce correct results regardless of the number of items in the sequence or the type of numbers (integers, floats or complex numbers) in question.
In essence, a good program produces the expected results at all times.

There are times when you think that your program is working correctly only for it to break with unanticipated inputs.

Pro Tip:
It's worth noting that even experienced programmers don't always get their programs working on the first attempt.

Therefore, to ensure that your program is consistent in producing expected results, testing is needed. This can be accomplished manually by providing a variety of inputs and verifying if the resulting outputs align with the expected results.

This is not only tiring but error-prone. A better alternative would be to automate the process using testing tools available in Python.

Unit Testing

A program is typically composed of various units or building blocks that work together to accomplish a specific task. These units could be functions, methods, or even small sections of your code.

To determine if the program is functioning as intended, you can employ a technique called unit testing.

Unit testing is a software testing technique where individual units or components of a program are isolated and tested in isolation to verify their correctness.

By investing time in writing effective unit tests, you can build robust and reliable code that is easier to maintain and extend.

Interestingly, Python provides a variety of testing frameworks and tools to perform tests. One of the most popular testing frameworks for Python is unittest, which is part of Python's standard library.

Unittest Module

The unittest module in Python is a built-in testing framework that provides a set of tools and classes for writing and executing unit tests.

However, it's important to note that before you can actually conduct a unit test using the unittest module, you need to have some code that you want to test. This means you should have implemented the specific functions or methods that you want to verify.

Now, let's use the unittest module to perform a unit test in the following code:

```
class Number:
    def __init__(self, val):
        #define and assign values to the instance variable
```

```
        self.value = val

    def add(self, val):
        #perform addition and result result
        result = self.value + val
        return result

    def subtract(self, val):
        #perform subtraction and return result
        result =  self.value - val
        return result

    def multiply(self, val):
        #perform multiplication and return result
        result = self.value * val
        return result

    def divide(self, val):
        #perform division and return result
        result = self.value / val
        return result
```

This class contains four methods and these methods are designed to perform basic arithmetic operations including addition, subtraction, multiplication and division.

Each of these methods acts as a separate unit within the program. To conduct a unit test, you need to test each method individually to ensure their functionality and accuracy.

For example, the addition method could be tested by providing different input numbers and verifying that the returned result matches the expected sum. Similarly, the subtraction, multiplication, and division methods would be tested with appropriate input values to validate their accuracy.

To perform a unit test on this class, simply follow the steps outlined below:

1. Import the unittest module:
2. Create a test class (or TestCase) that inherits from unittest.TestCase.
3. Define test methods within the test class with each test method starting with the word "test".

4. Within each test method, write the test logic and use the assertion methods available in the unittest.TestCase class to verify if the expected result aligns with the actual result.
5. Finally, run the test case(s) by calling unittest.main() to execute the tests.

Once you follow the steps mentioned above, you'll be able to write unit tests for the Numbers class.

Here's an example of how you can do it:

```python
import unittest
class NumberTestCase(unittest.TestCase):
    def test_add(self):
        #testing the add method
        number = Number(10)
        val = 10
        output = 20
        result = number.add(val)
        self.assertEqual(result, output)

    def test_subtract(self):
        #testing the subtract method
        number = Number(10)
        val = 10
        output = 0
        result = number.subtract(val)
        self.assertEqual(result, output)

    def test_multiply(self):
        #testing the multiply method
        number = Number(10)
        val = 10
        output = 100
        result = number.multiply(val)
        self.assertEqual(result, output)

    def test_divide(self):
        #testing the divide method
        number = Number(10)
        val = 10
```

```
        output = 1
        result = number.divide(val)
        self.assertEqual(result, output)

#running the unit tests
unittest.main()
```

When you run this test, it will execute all the test methods within the NumberTestCase class. The test results will be displayed, indicating whether each test has passed or failed.

This way, you can easily see the outcome of each individual test and determine if the functionality of the Number class is working as expected.

Assertion Methods

Assertion methods are built-in functions provided by the unittest module that allow you to make assertions or statements about the expected behavior of your code.

These methods provide a way for you to validate whether the actual output or behaviour of your code matches your expectations. They compare the expected result with the actual result and raise an assertion error if they do not match.

Here are some commonly used assertion methods in the unittest module:

assertEqual(a, b): Checks if the values of a and b are equal.
assertTrue(expr): Checks if the expression expr evaluates to True.
assertFalse(expr): Checks if the expression expr evaluates to False.
assertIs(a, b): Checks that a is identical to b.
assertIsNot(a, b): Checks that a is not identical to b.
assertIn(a, b): Checks if a is a member of b.
assertNotIn(a, b): Checks that a is not a member of b.

Summary

This chapter started by explaining the importance of testing in the software development process. You learnt how to write code that is easily testable. You wrote tests using the unittest module, which is a built-in testing framework in Python.

Practice Exercises

1. What is unit testing and why is it important?
2. What do you understand by test-driven development?
3. How do you create a test suite with unittest module?
4. What are the commonly used assertion methods in unittest module?

## Chapter 17

ASYNCHRONOUS PROGRAMMING WITH ASYNCIO

"How much of human life is lost in waiting."
- Ralph Waldo Emerson

Have you ever been in a team where tasks had to be performed in a specific order, and sometimes you had to wait for someone to finish their tasks before you could proceed with yours? It can be quite frustrating when you have to put your work on hold just because someone else is not yet done with their part. Even if the person is not actively working on their task, you still have to wait until they are completely finished before you can continue with your own task. What if there was a way to utilize those waiting periods by doing something productive? In programming, it is called concurrency. It allows tasks to be executed simultaneously, meaning that we can perform other actions while waiting for certain tasks to complete. In Python, the asyncio module provides a way to achieve concurrency.

Learning outcome

In this chapter, you will learn:
- The fundamental concepts of asynchronous programming.
- To work with the asyncio library.
- To define and execute coroutines using the async and await keywords.
- To schedule and manage tasks in event loops.

Introduction

Typically, when a computer runs a program, it goes through the instructions one by one, from the top to the bottom. It completes each task before moving on to the next one. So, if there's a statement being executed, it won't allow the next statement to run until it finishes what it's doing. This is called synchronous programming.

Now, there's another way of programming called asynchronous programming. It allows the computer to perform different tasks simultaneously without one task blocking the others. This is particularly useful when you're dealing with a lot of network calls or similar situations.

In synchronous programming, tasks have to follow a strict order. They need to be executed one after another. But with asynchronous programming, you can have multiple tasks happening concurrently.

This means that while one task is being worked on, you can start processing another task that's ready to go. You can initiate multiple tasks and proceed to the next line of code without waiting for each task to complete.

By taking advantage of the Python's asyncio module, you can effectively write and manage asynchronous tasks effectively.

The asyncio module

The asyncio module also known as Asynchronous I/O is a powerful framework for writing asynchronous programs in Python. It allows you to write concurrent programs by using coroutines, event loops, and non-blocking I/O operations.

This means that if you have I/O operations like reading from a file or making a network request, instead of just waiting around for them to finish, the event loop in your program can keep doing other tasks in the meantime.

This way, your program becomes more efficient because it can make progress on other coroutines while waiting for the I/O operations to complete.

The following are the key components of asyncio module:

1. Coroutines
2. Event loops
3. Tasks
4. Futures
5. Event handlers

Coroutines

A coroutine is a special type of function that can be paused and resumed during execution. You define a coroutine by using the async keyword before the function declaration.

Pro Tip:
Coroutines are like normal functions except that they start with the keyword async.

Take a look at this example:

```
import asyncio
async def greet():
```

```
    print("Hello there!")
coro = greet()
```

The above example is a coroutine that does a simple task of displaying the message "Hello there!". By assigning the coroutine to the variable "coro," you can conveniently refer to it using this name.

To execute the coroutine, you can use the asyncio.run() function as shown below.

```
asyncio.run(greet())
```

Output:
Hello there!

Event Loop

The event loop is the heart of asyncio and is responsible for executing coroutines and managing tasks. It can be considered a message queue that processes tasks in a non-blocking manner.

The event loop continuously runs and waits for tasks to complete or for new events to occur. It manages the scheduling and execution of multiple coroutines concurrently.

In order to run a coroutine, you'll need to set up an event loop. To create an event loop, you can use the new_event_loop() function of the asyncio module.

```
# Create an event loop
loop = asyncio.new_event_loop()
```

This function creates a new event loop and with this event loop, you can run your coroutines within it.

```
# Run the coroutine within the event loop
loop.run_until_complete(coro)
```

By calling the loop.run_until_complete() function, you are instructing the event loop to ensure that the coroutine is completed within the loop.

Finally, the loop.close() is used to close the event loop to release any resources associated with it.

```
# Close the event loop
loop.close()
```

The await keyword

The await keyword is used within coroutines to indicate points where a coroutine can be suspended temporarily, allowing other concurrent operations to execute.

When an await expression is encountered within a coroutine, the coroutine willingly gives control back to the event loop, which acts like a message queue.

The event loop can then schedule and run other coroutines. Once the awaited operation finishes, the coroutine is picked up again from where it paused, allowing it to continue its execution smoothly.

```
async def greeting():
    print("Hello there!")
    await asyncio.sleep(1)
    print('How are you?')

coro = greeting()
loop = asyncio.new_event_loop()
loop.run_until_complete(coro)
loop.close()
```

When the greeting() coroutine is executed, it prints "Hello there!" and then encounters the await statement. At this point, it yields control back to the event loop to continue processing other tasks.

The asyncio.sleep(1) is an asynchronous sleep function that suspends the execution of the coroutine for 1 second without blocking the event loop.

Once the 1-second delay is complete, the greeting() coroutine resumes execution and prints "How are you?" before completing.

Output:

Hello there!
How are you?

> **Pro Tip:**
> *You are not limited to using only one await statement within your coroutines. You can have as many await statements as needed.*

```python
async def greet():
    print("Hi!")
    await asyncio.sleep(1)
    print("Hello!")
    await asyncio.sleep(2)
    print("How are you?")
```

Having multiple await statements allows you to write coroutines that can perform multiple asynchronous operations concurrently.

Each await statement represents a point where the coroutine temporarily suspends its execution and allows other tasks to run.

Tasks

A task represents a coroutine scheduled for execution in the event loop. It keeps track of the progress of the coroutine and ensures that it is properly scheduled and resumed when needed.

Tasks can be created using the create_task() function, which schedules the coroutine to run in the event loop.

```python
async def main():
    task = asyncio.create_task(coro)
    result = await task
    print(result)
```

You can monitor or even cancel the task using task.cancel() function or keep the coroutine running until it is completed using loop.run_until_complete() function.

```
loop = asyncio.new_event_loop()
loop.run_until_complete(main())
```

Also, you can group tasks to work continuously together using asyncio.gather().

```
async def main():
    results = await asyncio.gather(coro, coro)
    print(results)
```

Futures

A future represents a task that is happening in the background that allows you to know when it is completed. Instead of constantly monitoring it, you can relax and be rest assured that it will notify you once it's finished.

Let's say you have a program that needs to download a large file from the internet. You create a future, and while the file is being downloaded, your program can continue doing other things. When the download is completed, the future will hold the downloaded file, allowing you to access it whenever you need it.

Future objects represent the eventual outcome of an asynchronous operation and act as placeholders for results that will be available in the future.

Futures can be used to chain coroutines together or to wait for multiple coroutines to complete concurrently.

Take a look at this example:

```
async def greeting(future):
    await asyncio.sleep(1)
    result = "Hello there!"
    future.set_result(result)

async def main():
    loop = asyncio.get_event_loop()
    fut = loop.create_future()
```

```
    loop.create_task(greeting(fut))
    await fut
    print(fut.result())

loop = asyncio.new_event_loop()
loop.run_until_complete(main())
```

In the above example, the greeting() function uses future.set_result(result) to assign the result to the future. In the main() function, an event loop is obtained using loop = asyncio.get_event_loop().

A future object is created using fut = loop.create_future() to hold the result of the greeting. Then, a task is created with loop.create_task(greeting(fut)) to execute the greeting() function asynchronously. The execution pauses at await fut until the future is completed.

Finally, the result of the future is printed using print(fut.result()).

Fetching multiple images in a website using asyncio

Now, let's create a simple program that can fetch multiple images from a website all at once using the asyncio module.

```
import requests
import asyncio


def fetch_image(url):
    response = requests.get(url)
    return response.content
async def download_images(urls):
    loop = asyncio.get_event_loop()
    tasks = []
    for url in urls:
        task = loop.run_in_executor(None, fetch_image, url)
        tasks.append(task)
    images = await asyncio.gather(*tasks)
    return images
```

```python
async def main():
    image_urls = [
            "https://images.pexels.com/photos/1595104/pexels-
            photo-1595104.jpeg",

            "https://images.pexels.com/photos/221016/pexels-
            photo-221016.jpeg",

            "https://images.pexels.com/photos/348689/pexels-
            photo-348689.jpeg"
    ]
    images = await download_images(image_urls)
    for i, image in enumerate(images, start=1):
        filename = f"image{i}.jpg"
        with open(filename, "wb") as file:
            file.write(image)
        print(f"Downloaded {filename}")


loop = asyncio.new_event_loop()
loop.run_until_complete(main())
```

This example makes use of two libraries: requests and asyncio.

The requests library helps with handling HTTP requests, while asyncio is used for managing tasks that can run asynchronously.

Now, there's a function called fetch_image(url). Its purpose is to take a URL as input and retrieve the content of an image from that URL. So, it basically fetches the image data.

The download_images(urls) function is asynchronous and the purpose is to create a separate task for each URL in the list provided.

By using run_in_executor, the event loop delegates the execution of the fetch_image function to a separate executor, allowing it to run concurrently with other tasks in the event loop. This helps prevent blocking the event loop and ensures that the downloading of images can happen concurrently.

Lastly, the main() function, which is also an asynchronous, awaits the result of the download_images() function. This means that it waits until all the images are downloaded before moving on to any further instructions.

Summary

You learnt fundamental concepts of asynchronous programming and learnt how to work with the asyncio library in Python. You learnt how to define and execute coroutines using the async and await keywords. Also, you learnt how to schedule and manage tasks in event loops.

Practice Exercises

1. What is asynchronous programming?
2. What are the benefits of asynchronous programming?
3. What is asyncio module used for?
4. What is an event loop?
5. How do you create a coroutine?
6. Explain the function of the await keyword?
7. Write a program that downloads multiple images from the internet using asyncio.

Chapter 18

RESUESTS IN PYTHON

"A clever, imaginative, humorous request can open closed doors and closed minds."

- Percy Ross

When it comes to accessing and sending information over the internet, we often rely on browsers to do the job. Browsers have become the go-to tool for browsing websites, retrieving data, and interacting with online services. However, as a programmer, you can write a program that can fetch or send any information you want without having to use a browser. In Python, there are several ways to accomplish this, but one of the most popular and user-friendly option is using the requests library.

Learning outcome

In this chapter, you will learn:
- Basic concepts of the Hypertext Transfer Protocol (HTTP).
- The different HTTP methods - GET, POST, PUT and DELETE.
- To install the requests library and import into your programs.
- To construct URLs, include query parameters, and handle responses.
- To extract data from the responses and parse JSON.

The Requests library is a popular Python library that simplifies the process of making HTTP requests and interacting with websites. It allows you to write programs that can send requests to a website and receive responses from it.

With this library, you can initiate various types of HTTP requests, such as GET, POST, PUT and DELETE.

For example, if you want to get some information from a website, you can use a GET request to instruct the web server to give you the information.

Once you send the request, the web server will respond with the information, and you can then do whatever you want with it in your program.

To use the requests library in Python, you need to have it installed on your computer. Since it is not a part of the Python standard library, you are required to install it separately by running the following command in your terminal:

```
pip install requests
```

Once the installation is complete, you can start using the requests library by importing it into your program.

```
import requests
```

Making a GET request

A GET request is generally used to retrieve data or information from a specific resource on a server. It can be a web page, an image, a file, or any other type of resource that is accessible via a URL.

With the Requests library, you can easily make GET requests or fetch data from a specific URL using the requests.get() function.

```
#send a GET request
response = requests.get('https://example.com')
```

The requests.get() function initiates the GET request to the specified URL and returns a response object. This response object represents the response received from the server after sending the request.

By assigning the returned response object to the variable response, you can store and access the information provided by the server in your program.

Accessing the content of the response

The response object contains various properties and methods that allow you to access and handle the server's response.

For example, you can use response.status_code to retrieve the status code of the response, response.text to access the response content as a string, response.json() to parse the response as JSON, and response.headers to access the response headers.

The example below demonstrates how you can retrieve various pieces of information from a response object.

```
#check the status
status = response.status_code
```

```python
print(status)

#get content
content = response.text
print(content)

#get headers
headers = response.headers
print(headers['Content-Type'])
```

In the above example, the status code of the response is retrieved and stored in the variable status. By printing status, you can see the code and determine if the request was successful or if there were any errors. or instance.

Pro Tip:
A status code of 200 means the request was successful.

By assigning response.text to the variable content and printing it, you can view the actual data received from the server.

Also, the response.headers provides a dictionary-like object that contains the headers sent by the server in the response.

Outputs:
200

```
<!doctype html>
<html>
<head>
<title>Example Domain</title>

<meta charset="utf-8" />
<meta http-equiv="Content-type" content="text/html; charset=utf-8" />
<meta name="viewport" content="width=device-width, initial-scale=1" />
<style type="text/css">
  body {
    background-color: #f0f0f2;
    margin: 0;
    padding: 0;
```

```
        font-family: -apple-system, system-ui, BlinkMacSystemFont, "Segoe UI", "Open Sans",
  "Helvetica Neue", Helvetica, Arial, sans-serif;

    }
    div {
      width: 600px;
      margin: 5em auto;
      padding: 2em;
      background-color: #fdfdff;
      border-radius: 0.5em;
      box-shadow: 2px 3px 7px 2px rgba(0,0,0,0.02);
    }
    a:link, a:visited {
      color: #38488f;
      text-decoration: none;
    }
    @media (max-width: 700px) {
      div {
        margin: 0 auto;
        width: auto;
      }
    }
  }
</style>
</head>

<body>
<div>
<h1>Example Domain</h1>
<p>This domain is for use in illustrative examples in documents. You may use this
    domain in literature without prior coordination or asking for permission.</p>
<p><a href="https://www.iana.org/domains/example">More information...</a></p>
</div>
</body>
</html>

text/html; charset=UTF-8
```

Passing query strings in GET requests

Query strings are used to specify additional information or data that you want to send to the server as part of the request.

To pass query strings in a GET request, you can append them to the URL using the params parameter of the requests.get() function.The params parameter is passed as a dictionary, and each key-value pair in the dictionary represents a query parameter.

Here's an example of how to pass query parameters in a GET request using requests:

```
# Send the GET request with the query parameters
query = {
    'key1': 'value 1',
    'key2': 'value 2',
}
response = requests.get(url, params=query)
```

Sending a POST request

The POST method is commonly used to submit data to a server for processing or to create a new resource. With the requests.post() function of the requests library, you can send a POST request.

```
# Sending the POST request
url = 'https://example.com'

data = {
    'key1': 'value1',
    'key2': 'value2'
}
response = requests.post(url, data=data)
```

In this example, the URL and data arguments refer to the page where you want to send the request to and the data you want to send. The function returns a Response object that contains the server's response to the request.

JSON contents

JSON is a simple and readable way to represent and exchange data. It serves as a standardized data interchange format allowing systems and applications to exchange structured data seamlessly.

JSON is lightweight, meaning that it doesn't use a lot of space or resources, making it efficient for sending data over the internet.

Interestingly, the requests library provides convenient methods to interact with JSON data. For instance, you can use the json() method to automatically parse the response from an API call into a JSON object.

```python
# URL of the API endpoint
url = 'https://api.example.com'

# Sending a GET request
response = requests.get(url)

#fetching JSON contents
    json_data = response.json()
    print(json_data)
```

Similarly, you can use the json parameter when sending a request to automatically convert a Python dictionary or list into JSON before sending it.

```python
# URL of the API endpoint
url = 'https://api.example.com'

# JSON data to send in the request body
data = {
    'key1': 'value1',
    'key2': 'value2'
}
# Sending a POST request
response = requests.post(url, json=data)
```

Sending files

The request library allows you to include files as part of a POST request. To do this, you are required to provide the file's path, which is the location on your computer where the file is stored.

To send the POST request with the file, you'll open the file in binary mode using the open() function, and then use the requests.post() function to send the file.

Inside the requests.post() function, you'll include the files parameter and provide a dictionary with the file object as the value.

```
# URL of where you want to send the POST request
url = 'https://example.com'

# File to send in the request
file_path = 'data.txt'

# Sending the POST request with the file
with open(file_path, 'rb') as file:
    files = {'file': file}
    response = requests.post(url, files=files)
```

Sessions

A session is basically a series of interaction or communication between a client (such as a web browser or a program) and a server. During a session, the client and server maintain a connection and exchange information, allowing the client to access and retrieve various resources from the server.

The session between the client and server remains active as long as they keep exchanging information. This allows the client to continue making requests and receiving responses from the server, thereby making the browsing experience more seamless and effic ient.

Creating a Session

To work with sessions in the Requests library, you have to create a Session object.

```
# Create a session
```

```
session = requests.Session()
```

Once you have the session object, you can start making requests. You can use it to send HTTP requests just like you would with requests.get() or requests.post().

The only difference is that you use the methods of the session object, such as session.get() or session.post().

```
# Send a GET request using the session
response = session.get('https://example.com/')
```

This object acts as a central point for handling all the communication between your program and the server.

When you are done with your requests, it's a good practice to close the session when you're done. You can close a session by calling the session.close() method.

```
# Close the session
session.close()
```

Response Headers

Headers are like special instructions or pieces of information that you can attach to your requests. They can contain things like authentication tokens, user-agent information, or any other custom details you want to send along with your request.

To access the response headers, you can use the response.headers attribute, which returns a dictionary-like object containing the headers. By examining the response headers, you can retrieve information such as content type, server information, caching directives, authentication-related headers, and more.

```
# Send a GET request
response = requests.get('https://example.com)

# Access the response headers
```

```
headers = response.headers
# Print all the headers
# Access specific headers
content_type = headers.get('content-type')
server = headers.get('server')

# Print specific headers
print(f"Content-Type: {content_type}")
print(f"Server: {server}")
```

In addition to the headers that are automatically included in an HTTP request, you also have the ability to create your own custom headers. This means you can add your own personalized instructions or details to the request.

You can do this by providing a dictionary with the header key-value pairs to the headers parameter.

Here's an example of how to create and send a request with custom headers:

```
# Custom headers
headers = {
    'User-Agent': 'Custom User Agent',
    'Authorization': 'Token',
    'Custom-Header': 'Value'
}

# Send a GET request with custom headers
response = requests.get('https://example.com', headers=headers)
```

In this case, the 'User-Agent', 'Authorization', and 'Custom-Header' are included in the headers.

Timeouts

When making HTTP requests, it's important to set timeouts to prevent the request from hanging indefinitely and to have control over the maximum time to wait for a response from the server.

For instance, a connection timeout specifies the maximum amount of time to wait for the server to establish a connection. If the connection cannot be established within the specified timeout, a requests.exceptions.ConnectTimeout exception is raised.

```
# Set read timeout to 10 seconds
timeout = 5
response = requests.get('https://example.com', timeout=timeout)
```

In this example, a connection timeout of 5 seconds is set using the timeout parameter of the requests.get() method. If the server doesn't respond within the specified timeout duration, a ConnectTimeout exception is raised.

Summary

This chapter began by explaining how to make HTTP requests. You learnt how install and use the requests library in your programs. Also, you learnt how to construct URLs, include query parameters, and handle responses. Finally, you learnt how to extract data from the responses and parse JSON.

Practice Exercises

1. What is the purpose of the requests library?
2. Mention 5 HTTP request methods.
3. What is the difference between a GET and POST request?
4. Write a program to send a request to a web page and print the header information. Write a program to send a request to a web page and print the JSON value of the response.
5. Write a program to send a request to a web page and stop waiting for a response after a given number of seconds.
6. Write a program to send some data in the URL query string
7. Write the difference between GET and POST methods

Chapter 19

WEB SCRAPPING IN PYTHON

"He who does not see things in their depth should not call himself a radical."
- Jose Marti

Having learnt how to write programs that can get or send requests to web pages, the next exciting step is to learn how to fetch or extract specific information from websites. We can retrieve things like stock prices, news headlines, or even product reviews without relying on our browsers. Instead of manually browsing through websites, we can automate the process and retrieve the desired information. This process is known as web scrapping.

Learning outcome

In this chapter, you will learn:
- To use Beautiful Soup to parse HTML content.
- To traverse and navigate through web pages.
- To Locate specific elements or information.
- To save extracted data to files (CSV or databases).
- The ethical considerations in web scrapping.

Introduction

Web scraping is the process of collecting data from the internet using methods other than the conventional web browser.

Imagine you have a list of websites, and you want to gather specific data from each of them, like the prices of products or the latest news headlines. Instead of manually going to each website and copying the data, you can write a program that does this task for you automatically. This process of fetching this information from these websites is known as web scrapping.

With the emergence of data-driven decision-making, web scraping has emerged as a powerful technique for extracting valuable information from websites. It is widely used in machine learning, business forecasting, medical reporting and diagnostics and so on.

Interestingly, Python has several libraries and tools that make web scraping tasks a lot easier. These libraries provide helpful functions and tools to simplify tasks like fetching web pages, parsing HTML code, and extracting data.

There are several popular libraries used for web scraping in Python. However, BeautifulSoup and Scrapy are widely used and quite popular among developers.

Beautiful Soup Library

Beautiful Soup provides a convenient way to extract data from HTML and XML documents, making it easier for developers to parse and navigate through the structure of web pages.

It provides an intuitive interface to navigate and search the parsed data, making it a suitable option for beginners.

In order to do some web scraping using BeautifulSoup, you'll need to make sure you have it installed on your system. Additionally, if you want to follow along with this book, it's recommended to install the requests library as well.

> **Pro Tip:**
> *When you want to scrape data from a website, you need to access the web page's content. That's where the requests library comes in. It helps you send HTTP requests to the website and retrieve the web page's HTML code.*

Once you have the HTML code of the web page, BeautifulSoup jumps into action. It takes that raw HTML code and makes it easy for you to navigate, search, and extract the specific data you're interested in.

Using the pip, you can install these libraries by running the following commands:

```
pip install beautifulsoup4
pip install requests
```

Once you have successfully installed BeautifulSoup and Requests, you are all set for web scraping.

However, before delving deeper into scrapping, it is important that you understand the workflow for web scrapping.

Basic Web Scraping Workflow with BeautifulSoup

The basic workflow for web scraping using BeautifulSoup involves a few key steps:

1. Inspect the website's HTML structure

Inspecting the HTML structure of a website allows you to locate the data you want to scrape by identifying the relevant elements and their attributes.

If you want to understand the HTML structure of a web page you want to scrape, you can use the developer tools in popular web browsers like Google Chrome or Mozilla Firefox.

2. Fetch the web page

Having understood how a web page is organized, you can proceed with retrieving it. By retrieving the page, you essentially acquire all the HTML, CSS, JavaScript, and additional resources that compose the web page.

Let's say that you want to extract some data from the Wikipedia homepage. Using the Requests library, you can send an HTTP request to the website and retrieve the HTML content.

```
#fetch page
url = 'https://www.wikipedia.org/'
response = requests.get(url)
```

3. Parse the HTML

After obtaining the content of the web page, the next step is to analyze and extract meaningful information from the HTML. Using the BeautifulSoup. you can traverse the HTML tree structure and extract specific elements or data.

However, before employing BeautifulSoup's functionalities, it is necessary to create a BeautifulSoup object. This requires you to provide the HTML code of the web page as the first argument and the desired HTML parser, such as "html.parser," as the second argument.

```
#parse html
soup = BeautifulSoup(response.content, "html.parser")
```

The first argument represents the HTML code of the web page, which can typically be accessed using the "response.content" attribute, while the second argument specifies the HTML parser that BeautifulSoup will use to parse and understand the HTML code.

Pro Tip:
HTML parser is a tool or library that transforms raw HTML code into a structured representation, typically a Document Object Model (DOM).

In this particular case, the specified parser is "html.parser"which is a default option included in Python's standard library.

4. Extract the desired data

Once you've created a BeautifulSoup object, you can then proceed to extract the desired information from the web page.

BeautifulSoup provides a variety of methods that facilitate this extraction process. For example, you can use methods like find() or find_all() to locate elements based on their tags, attributes, or other criteria. You can even narrow down your search and retrieve the desired elements.

The example below shows how you can extract and print the content of all the paragraph elements from a BeautifulSoup object.

```
#extract data
pgs = soup.find_all("p")
for pg in pgs:
    print(pg)
```

5. Store or process the data

Once you've extracted the data, you can save it to a file, store it in a database, or process it further for analysis or visualization.

Pro Tip:
Python has wide support for so many databases including MySQL, Oracle, PostgreSQL, SQLite and so many others.

BeautifulSoup Methods and attributes

Beautiful Soup provides several methods and attributes that enable users to perform various tasks on documents. These methods are designed to search for specific elements within documents.

Tags

Beautiful Soup enables you to work with a range of popular HTML tags, including <div>, <p>, <a>, <img>, <ul>, <ol>, <li>, <table>, <tr>, <th>, <td>, <h1> through <h6>, <span>, <form>, <input>, and <button>.

You can search for elements based on these tags using methods like find() and find_all(), and then access attributes, text content, or manipulate the elements.

find() method

This method allows you to search for the first occurrence of a specified HTML tag or a combination of tags, attributes, or text within a document.

```
# Find the first occurrence of a h1 tag
soup.find("h1")

# Find a h2 tag with an id="main"
soup.find("h2", id="main")

# Find a specific text within the document
soup.find(text="text to find")
```

find_all() method

This method searches for all occurrences of a specified tag or a combination of tags, attributes, or text. Instead of returning just the first occurrence, it scans the entire HTML document and retrieves all matching elements that meet the specified criteria.

```
# Find all occurrences of a h2
soup.find_all("h2")
```

```
# Find all h3 tags with id of main
soup.find_all("h3", id="main")
# Find all occurrences of a specific text
soup.find_all(text="text to find")
```

select() method

The select() method allows you to use CSS selectors for searching and selecting specific elements within an HTML document. By using CSS selectors with this method, you can apply more advanced and specific filtering techniques to narrow down your search and extract the desired elements from the web page.

For example, with CSS selectors, you can search for elements based on their tag names, classes, IDs, attributes, or even their hierarchical relationships.

```
# Select all elements with class "colour"
elements = soup.select(".colour")
# Select the element with ID "main"
element = soup.select("#main")
# Select all <a> tags within a <div> element with class "container"
links = soup.select("div.container a")
```

get() method

The get() method in Beautiful Soup allows you to retrieve the value of a specific attribute from an HTML tag.

For instance, an <a> tag may have an href attribute that holds the URL of a link, or an <img> tag may have a src attribute indicating the image source.

With the get() method, you can easily retrieve the value of a specific attribute from an HTML tag. You simply pass the name of the attribute as an argument to the method, and it returns the corresponding value.

```
# get the value of the 'href' attribute
link = soup.find('a')
href_text = link.get('href')
```

```
print("URL:", href_text)

# get the 'class' attribute of an element
element = soup.find('div')
class_value = element.get('class')
print(class_value)
```

The text attribute

The text attribute is used to retrieve the text content within a tag, excluding any HTML tags or markup. When you retrieve the text attribute of an HTML element, you get only the plain text that appears within that element, without any HTML tags, attributes, or formatting.

This can be useful when you are interested in extracting the textual content of a specific element without the noise of surrounding HTML code.

```
tags = soup.find_all("a")
for tag in tags:
    tag_text = tag.text
    print(tag_text)
```

Navigating the trees

When you parse a document with Beautiful Soup, it creates a special tree-like structure that represents the hierarchy of tags in the document. You can start by directly accessing specific tags using methods like find() or find_all().

But that's not all!

You can also venture upwards to the parent tag using the .parent attribute. It's like taking a step up the tag hierarchy.

The .children attribute lets you iterate over the direct child tags of a tag. It's like meeting and interacting with the "kids" of a tag, one by one.

In addition, you can use the .next_sibling attribute to retrieve the next sibling tag of a given tag. It's like getting to know the "brothers" or "sisters" of a tag.

Parent

The parent attribute allows you to navigate up the document tree and access the parent element of a given element. It allows you to navigate up the document tree and access the immediate parent element of a particular element.

Here is an example of how to use the parent attribute to find the parent element of an HTML element.

```
html = '''
<html>
<div id="part1">
<p>Paragraph 1</p>
<p>Paragraph 2</p>
</div>
<div id="part2">
<p>Paragraph 3</p>
<p>Paragraph 4</p>
<p>Paragraph 5</p>
</div>
</html>
'''
```

```
# Create a BeautifulSoup object
soup = BeautifulSoup(html, 'html.parser')
# Find the first <p> element
p1 = soup.find_all('p')[0]

# Access the parent element
pe = p1.parent

print("Current element:", p1)
print("Parent element:", pe)
```

By using the parent attribute, you can find the parent element of the first <p> tag, which contains the text "Paragraph 1". If you run this code, you will get the following outputs.

Current element: <p>Paragraph 1</p>
Parent element: <div id="part1">
<p>Paragraph 1</p>
<p>Paragraph 2</p>
</div>

Children

Children refers to the direct child elements of a given element within an HTML or XML document. It represents the elements that are directly contained within the given element.

The children elements of an element can be accessed using the children attribute in BeautifulSoup. This attribute allows you to iterate over the immediate child elements of a particular element.

Here's an example to illustrate the usage of the children attribute in BeautifulSoup:

```
# Create a BeautifulSoup object
soup = BeautifulSoup(html, "html.parser")
pe = soup.find('div', {'id': 'part1'})
```

The find() method is used to locate the first <div> element with the id attribute equal to "part1" within the HTML document. It takes the element type ('div') and a dictionary specifying the attribute-value pair ('id': 'part1') as arguments. The result is stored in the variable pe.

You can then iterate over the child elements of the <div> element (pe) found in the previous step.

```
# Iterate over the child elements
for child in pe.children:
    print(child)
```

If you run this code, you will get the following outputs.

<p>Paragraph 1</p>
<p>Paragraph 2</p>

Sibling

Beautiful Soup provides attributes like .next_sibling and .previous_sibling to access and retrieve the next and previous sibling tags of a given tag.

For instance, the next_sibling allows you to retrieve the next sibling tag of a given tag. It's like getting the tag that comes right after the current tag at the same level in the document's structure.

```python
# Find the first <p> element
p = soup.find('p')

# Get the next sibling element
next_sibling = p.next_sibling
```

Legal and Ethical Consideration in web scrapping

Web scrapping should be done in a responsible and ethical manner. Therefore, when engaging in this practice, it's essential to consider the legal and ethical implications.

Legality

Some websites explicitly prohibit scraping, while others may have specific rules or limitations. These rules are usually mentioned in the website's terms of service or terms of use, which explain how you can access and use their content. It's important to read and follow these rules to ensure you're using the website's data appropriately and legally.

Copyrights

Many times, the information you come across on the internet is protected by copyrights. This means that the person who created or owns that content has special rights to control how it is used and shared.

Because of these rights, you cannot copy or use someone else's work without their permission. It's important to be aware of copyright laws and respect them.

That's why it's important to give credit to the original source or get permission when necessary.

By doing so, you show respect for the creators' efforts and creativity, and you avoid any legal problems related to copyright infringement.

Therefore, ensure that you obtain permission, when necessary, respect copyright restrictions, and avoid scraping private or sensitive data without consent.

Data validation

A lot times, scrapped data may contain errors, inconsistencies, or irrelevant information due to variations in website structures or data quality. To ensure the accuracy and usefulness of the scraped data, it's essential to examine it carefully.

This means taking the time to review and analyze the information you have collected. By doing so, you can identify any errors or inconsistencies that may be present and make sure that the data you are using is reliable.

Attributions

When you use scraped data for any publication or analysis, it's considered good practice to give proper attribution to the original source. This means acknowledging and crediting the website or the owner of the data.

Proper attribution also fosters a culture of collaboration and encourages others to share their data openly. When you credit the original source, it can motivate others to provide more data in the future, benefiting the entire community.

Server loads

When you scrape data from a website, it's important to be mindful of the number and frequency of your requests. Sending too many requests in a short span of time can put excessive load on the server and affect its performance.

Therefore, it is important that you space out your requests and avoid overloading the server.

Summary

In this chapter, you learnt how to use the Beautiful Soup library in Python to extract data from HTML content. You learnt how to parse HTML content, navigate and locate specific elements and save extracted data to files in different formats (CSV, JSON, databases). Also, you learnt the ethical considerations involved in web scraping.

Practice Exercises

1. What is web scrapping?
2. Can you provide examples of when it is appropriate to scrape the web?
3. What are the pros and cons of web scrapping?
4. What steps do you take before scrapping?
5. Mention 3 libraries for web scrapping in Python?
6. What are the ethical responsibilities while scrapping a website?
7. Write a web crawler application using requests and BeautifulSoup.

LOGGING IN PYTHON

"Learn, compare, collect the facts!"

- Ivan Pavlov

Have you ever thought about the importance of monitoring your programs. Whether during development, testing, or in production, it is essential that you monitor your programs to ensure that it's running smoothly and performing as expected. By so doing, you can keep track of the program's performance, identify potential issues, and ensure it's functioning as expected. One way to monitor a program is by keeping track of certain events. It's like creating a log or record of important occurrences within the program. And by logging these events, we can have a record of what's happening, which can be beneficial for debugging or analyzing the program's behaviour later on.

Learning outcome

In this chapter, you will learn:
- The importance of logging in software development.
- To incorporate logging into your applications using the logging module.
- Various logging levels, such as DEBUG, INFO, WARNING, ERROR, and CRITICAL.
- To configure your log messages using timestamping and log levels.
- To direct log messages to different outputs, such as the console and files.

Introduction

Logging is a way to keep track of events that occur when a software program runs. It allows you to capture and record important information about what's happening behind the scenes.

By implementing proper logging practices, you can generate records of events, messages, warnings, and errors that occur during the program's execution. These logs act as a valuable source of information that helps you understand what exactly happened and where things might have gone wrong. It's like having a personal assistant keeping tabs on what's happening behind the scenes of your program.

Even when the program is deployed and running in a real-world environment, logging continues to play a crucial role as it allows you to monitor the program's behaviour, captures any unexpected events or errors, and gather insights about its performance.

Without proper logging records in place, it becomes much more difficult to identify and resolve issues that may arise.

Python comes with a built-in logging module that makes it really convenient to write status messages to files or any other output stream you prefer. This means you can choose where you want to store your logs, whether it's a file, console, or even a remote server.

Log levels

Log levels are used to categorize the severity or importance of log messages. They help developers understand the significance of each logged event.

Python provides several predefined log levels, including DEBUG, INFO, WARNING, ERROR, and CRITICAL.

The DEBUG is the lowest log level and is used for detailed messages that are primarily meant for developers during debugging and development. DEBUG-level messages provide information about the program's flow, variable values, and other fine-grained details.

The INFO level is used for general informational messages. It confirms that certain events or milestones in the program have occurred successfully. These messages help to understand the overall progress and state of the program during its execution.

WARNING indicate potential issues or unexpected behaviour that might not cause the program to fail but still require attention. It alerts you to potential problems or situations that could lead to errors or undesired outcomes.

The ERROR level indicates more severe issues that prevent the program from functioning correctly. When an error is logged, it signifies that a problem has occurred and needs to be addressed. It suggests that the program's execution might be affected or interrupted.

The CRITICAL level represents the highest severity level. It indicates critical errors or failures that might lead to the termination of the program or significant data loss. CRITICAL-level messages require immediate attention and typically represent severe and unexpected conditions.

By assigning the appropriate log level to each message, you can effectively categorize and prioritize the logged events based on their importance and impact on the program's execution.

Logging functions

Python's logging module offers a collection of functions that make it easier to log events without having to write extensive code.

These functions have names that correspond to the level or seriousness of the events they are meant to capture, simplifying most of the logging operations and they include:

- logging.debug()
- logging.info()
- logging.warning()
- logging.error()
- logging.critical()

Logging.debug() is used to provide detailed information, especially when diagnosing a problem.

Logging.info() is used to report events that occur during the normal operation of a program such as status monitoring or fault investigation.

Logging.warning() issues a warning regarding an unexpected runtime event.

Logging.error() is used to report an error preventing on or more functionality from working properly.

Logging.critical() is used to report serious error that can stop a program from running or to report when one or more key functionalities are not working and thereby affecting every other part of the system.

Creating and configuring the logger

To be able to generate logs using the logging module, you must first import the module.

```
import logging
```

Once you have imported the logging module, you gain access to the functions and classes available in the module.

This module provides a Logger class, which is the main component used to create loggers and generate log messages. With this class, you can configure the logging system based on your specific needs or preferences.

For example, you can write a message to show that your program is running smoothly (like an "INFO" message) or to indicate that something went wrong (like an "ERROR" message).

```
#configure logger
logging.basicConfig(level=logging.DEBUG)
logging.debug('This is a debug message')
logging.info('This is an info message')
logging.warning('This is a warning message')
logging.error('This is an error message')
logging.critical('This is a critical message')
```

Output:
DEBUG:root:This is a debug message
INFO:root:This is an info message
WARNING:root:This is a warning message
ERROR:root:This is an error message
CRITICAL:root:This is a critical message

If you run this code, the logged messages will be displayed on the console or terminal window, but you can also configure your logger to send the log messages to a file.

Logging to a file

Logging to a file allows you to maintain a persistent record of events and messages generated by your program. This record can be useful for troubleshooting issues, analyzing program behaviour, and reviewing the sequence of events leading up to a problem.

To ensure that the logging output is redirected to the specified file instead of being displayed on the console or terminal, you are required to provide a filename as part of the configuration.

```
#logging to a file
logging.basicConfig(filename='data.log', level=logging.DEBUG)
logging.warning('This is a warning message')
```

By providing filename with the value 'data.log', it specifies that the log messages will be written to a file named "data.log".

Formatting your messages

You can format your logged information to include relevant details such as timestamps, log levels, module names, or custom message fields.

For example, you can add timestamps to indicate when an event occurred, log levels to show the severity of the message, module names to identify the source of the log, or even custom message fields specific to your application. This is to ensure that the information presented is informative, easy to read, and follows a consistent pattern.

```
#logging with timestamps
logging.basicConfig(format='%(asctime)s %(message)s',
filename='data.log', level=logging.DEBUG)
logging.info('Logged a message.')

#logging with severity level
logging.basicConfig(format='%(levelname)s:%(message)s',
filename='data.log', level=logging.DEBUG)
logging.critical('This is critical.')

#logging with custom message
logging.basicConfig(format='%(message)s:%(message)s',
filename='data.log', level=logging.DEBUG)
logging.warning('This is a Warning!')
```

Tracking Program Execution with Logging

Logging allows you track important events, actions, and even errors that occur while your program runs. By writing these details to a log, you can later review and understand how your program behaves, which is super helpful for finding and fixing issues.

Now, let's take a look at a program that demonstrates how the logging module can be used.

This program uses the logging module to log various messages throughout the calculation process, starting from the beginning of the calculation, then recording the intermediate results, any errors that occur, and finally marking the completion of the calculations.

```python
# Configure the logger
logging.basicConfig(filename='data.log', level=logging.INFO,
format='%(asctime)s %(levelname)s: %(message)s')
def calculate(num1, num2):
    # Log an informational message
    logging.info('Calculation started...')

    try:
        result = num1/num2
        logging.info(f'{num1} divided by {num2} = {result}')
        logging.info('Done with division!')

    except Exception as e:
        # Log an error message
        logging.error(f'Error occurred: {str(e)}')

    # Log a final message
    logging.info('Done with calculations')

calculate(10, 2)
calculate(5, 0)
```

If you run this program, it will log records different events, messages and errors encountered during the calculations.

By examining the logged messages, you can get a clearer picture of how the code behaves, identify any problems that arise, and make the necessary adjustments to improve the program's performance and reliability.

Summary

This chapter began by explaining the importance of logging in software development. You learnt how to incorporate logging into your applications using the built-in logging module. You wrote programs that log messages with timestamps and log levels, direct log messages to consoles and files.

Practice Exercises

1. What is logging?

2. What is the purpose of the logging module?
3. State 5 logging levels and the relevance in software development lifecycle.
4. How do you configure a logger with basicConfig?
5. What are the various ways you can format Log messages?
6. Write a program that uses the logging module to display level name and message.
7. What are the advantages of logging over printing?

MULTITHREADING IN PYTHON

"The thing I lose patience with the most is the clock. Its hands move too fast."
- Thomas Edison

Have you ever noticed how we often multitask in our daily lives? Like when we listen to music or take a call while driving, we're doing more than one thing simultaneously. Multitasking is quite common, and it can be a real time-saver in certain situations. Although it's not always possible for every task, there are times when juggling multiple activities can be quite efficient. While multitasking can't be applied to every task, there are scenarios where it comes in handy. Interestingly, this concept is applicable in programming as well, and it's known as multithreading.

Learning outcome

In this chapter, you will learn:
- The concept of threads and their significance in programming.
- To use the threading module to create and manage threads
- To create and execute threads.
- Thread synchronization techniques.

Introduction

Imagine you've been assigned a massive project with numerous smaller tasks. If you were to tackle it alone, it would take a lot of time. You'd have to complete each task one by one, patiently moving on to the next only after finishing the previous one.

What if you were able to get the help of your friends?

This means that you could divide the tasks between yourselves and work together. This way, you both are doing different things at the same time, and would complete the project faster.

Think of multithreading as having little helpers called threads. These threads are like small workers inside a computer that can handle different tasks.

With multithreading, you can break down a big task into smaller pieces and assign each piece to a different thread. Each thread works independently, focusing on its specific part of the task.

By using multiple threads, your program gains the ability to simultaneously perform multiple tasks, resulting in enhanced speed and efficiency.

However, it's important to note that not all tasks can be done faster with multithreading. Some tasks, like solving a math problem, require a lot of thinking and don't benefit much from having multiple threads.

But tasks like downloading files from the internet or processing large amounts of data can be faster with multithreading because while one thread is waiting for data to arrive, other threads can continue working.

Writing multithreaded programs in Python

To create multithreaded programs in Python, you would need the 'threading' module. This module allows you to perform multiple tasks simultaneously.

By importing the threading module, you can leverage its functionality to implement multithreading in your program.

```
Import threading
```

One of the key features provided by the threading module is the Thread class. This class allows you to create and manage threads.

You can create a new thread by instantiating the Thread class from the threading module and providing it with a target function to execute. The target function defines the task that the thread will perform.

```
def task1():
    print('Task 1')

def task2():
    print('Task 2')

#creating threads
thread1 = threading.Thread(target=task1)
```

```
thread2 = threading.Thread(target=task2)
```

In this case, task1() and task2() are two functions representing the tasks you want the threads to execute.

Then, you can proceed to start the thread using the start() method.

```
#start the threads
thread1.start()
thread2.start()
```

By calling the start() method on the thread object, the task function will be executed concurrently in a separate thread of execution. This allows multiple threads to run simultaneously and perform different tasks in your program.

Typically, when a program starts running, it typically begins executing in a single thread called the main thread. This thread is created automatically by the operating system when the program is launched.

If the main program does not wait for the threads to finish their execution, it may continue running and potentially terminate before the threads have completed their tasks.

Therefore, to ensure that the main program waits for the completion of two separate, you can use the join() method.

When you call on the join() method on a thread, the main program will pause its execution and wait for that thread to finish its execution before proceeding further.

```
#wait for the threads to complete
thread1.join()
thread2.join()
print("All tasks completed")
```

Thread Synchronization

When you have multiple threads in a program, it means that different parts of the program are executing simultaneously. These threads might want to use or change the same resources or variables.

> **Pro Tip:**
> *A race condition occurs when two or more threads can access shared data and they try to change it at the same time, and do so in a way to cause unexpected results.*

Therefore, it's important to make sure that these threads work together smoothly without causing conflicts or racing against each other and this is where thread synchronization steps in.

Thread synchronization techniques are used to manage and control the interaction between threads. They ensure that the threads work together in a safe and orderly manner.

In Python, synchronization primitives such as locks, semaphores, and condition variables, are used to help coordinate access to shared data among multiple threads.

Locks

You can use lock to prevent multiple threads from modifying the value of the same variable at a time. This means that when a thread wants to modify the variable, it first acquires the lock.

Once the lock is acquired, the thread can safely perform its operations on the variable. If another thread tries to access the variable, it will have to wait until the lock is released by the first thread.

By creating a Lock object, you can ensure that only a single thread can make changes to the variable at any given time. This object allows threads to acquire and release the lock, ensuring exclusive access to the shared resource.

When a thread wants to use the resources, it acquires the lock, which means it holds the key and has exclusive access to the resources. This ensures that no other thread can use the resources at the same time and helps prevent conflicts.

To acquire a lock, you have to use the acquire() method of the Lock object.

```
# Create a lock object
lock = threading.Lock()
```

Once a thread has finished using the resources, it's important to release the lock.

Releasing the lock means giving up the key and allowing other threads to acquire it and use the resources.

To release the lock, you can use the release() method of the Lock object.

```
lock.release()
```

The following example demonstrates how you can use the acquire() and release() methods of the Lock object to admit students and update the population of students.

```
Import threading
students = {'population': 0}
counter = 1

# Lock for synchronization
lock = threading.Lock()

# Function to increment the population
def admit_student():
    global students
    global counter
    lock.acquire()
    print(f'Admitting student{counter}')
    students['population'] += 1
    print(f'Admitted student{counter}')
    #print separator lines
    print('-'*20)
    counter +=1
    lock.release()

# Creating multiple threads to admit students
threads = []
```

```
for _ in range(5):
    thread = threading.Thread(target=admit_student)
    threads.append(thread)
    thread.start()

for thread in threads:
    thread.join()

# Printing the updated population of students
print("Total number of students admitted:",
students['population'])
```

If you run this program, you will have the following outputs:

Admitting student1
Admitted student1

Admitting student2
Admitted student2

Admitting student3
Admitted student3

Admitting student4
Admitted student4

Admitting student5
Admitted student5

Total number of students admitted: 5

Daemon Threads

A daemon thread is a type of thread that runs in the background and does not prevent the program from exiting. Unlike regular threads, which must complete their execution before the program terminates, daemon threads are abruptly terminated when the main program exits.

The main distinction of daemon threads is that they are not required to complete their execution before the program exits. This makes them useful for tasks that need to run continuously in the background without blocking the program from terminating.

Here's an example that demonstrates the concept of daemon threads:

```
#daemon threads
import threading
import time

# Function executed by a daemon thread
def task():
    while True:
        print("Daemon thread is running")
        time.sleep(1)

# Create a daemon thread
thread = threading.Thread(target=task)
thread.daemon = True

# Start the daemon thread
thread.start()

# Main program continues executing
print("Main program is running")

# Sleep for some time to allow the daemon thread to run
time.sleep(5)

# The program exits without waiting for the daemon thread to
complete
print("Exiting the program")
```

By setting the daemon attribute to True, you mark the thread as a daemon thread. The task() function represents the task that the daemon thread executes, and in this case, it continuously prints a message every second.

The main program continues to execute alongside the daemon thread. After a brief delay, the program exits without waiting for the daemon thread to complete. As a result, the daemon thread is abruptly terminated when the main program exits.

Daemon threads are particularly useful for tasks such as background monitoring or periodic cleanups that can run independently. Since, a daemon thread will shut down immediately the program exits, you don't have to worry about shutting it down.

Difference between asyncio and threading

Asyncio and multithreading are two different approaches to achieving concurrent and asynchronous programming in Python.

The asyncio is based on the concept of event loops and coroutines. It uses a single thread to execute multiple tasks concurrently by switching between them when they are waiting for I/O operations to complete.

On the other hand, multithreading involves running multiple threads simultaneously, where each thread performs its own task independently. These threads can run in parallel on different CPU cores, allowing for true parallelism.

However, asyncio is suitable for applications with a high volume of I/O-bound tasks, where tasks spend most of their time waiting for I/O operations to complete. It is efficient and uses a single thread, making it ideal for scenarios like web servers or network clients.

Multithreading is suitable for CPU-bound tasks, where the computation itself takes up most of the processing time. It allows multiple threads to execute simultaneously, utilizing multiple CPU cores and speeding up program execution.

Global Interpreter Lock in Python (GIL)

The Global Interpreter Lock (GIL) is a mechanism that allows only one thread to execute Python instructions at a time, even on multicore systems. This means that, despite having multiple threads, only one thread can be actively running Python code at any given moment.

The implication of this on multithreading in Python is that it can limit the potential performance gains that are typically associated with using multiple threads.

Instead of achieving true parallelism, where multiple threads execute simultaneously on different CPU cores, the GIL enforces a form of concurrency called "thread interleaving."

This means that the threads take turns executing their instructions, with the GIL being periodically released to allow another thread to run.

The effect of the GIL is that CPU-bound tasks, which heavily rely on computational processing, may not observe significant performance improvements from multithreading due to the limitations imposed by the GIL.

Summary

In this chapter, you have learnt the importance of threads and their significance in programming. You learnt how to create and manage threads using the threading module in Python. Also, you learnt thread synchronization techniques to manage shared resources and avoid race conditions.

Practice Exercises

1. Explain the concept of threads in Python
2. What are the benefits of using multithreading in Python
3. What is the essence of locks in multithreading?
4. What is the difference between a process and a thread?
5. What is race condition in multithreading?
6. How do you understand by synchronization?
7. How does the GIL work?

PROPERTIES AND DESCRIPTORS

"I realised that what I loved was descriptive writing rather than something with a plot."
- Arlo Parks

Imagine this scenario: There's a store running a promotion, and they're offering a special discount to customers who have spent over $100 in their store within the past 30 days. Basically, if you've been a big spender in the store recently, you get a 20 percent discount on your purchases. But here's the thing, the store needs to keep track of all the transactions made by each customer over the last 30 days to figure out who qualifies for the discount. That's where properties and descriptors come into play. With this, the store can automate the process and accurately determine which customers are eligible for the discount based on their total spending.

Learning outcome

In this chapter, you will learn:
- To use properties to manage attribute access, validation, and manipulation.
- To use property decorators to simplify implementation of properties.
- To control attribute access, modification, and deletion using descriptors

Introduction

In object-oriented programming, objects play a vital role as the fundamental building blocks of programs. By creating an object, you are defining a specific instance of a class, which serves as a blueprint or template that object.

Objects are characterized by attributes, which act as variables holding information about the object's current state. and facilitate the storage and retrieval of relevant data. These attributes allow you to store and retrieve relevant data associated with the object.

By using the dot notation, you can access or modify the attributes of a given object or instances of the class.

Take a look at this example:

```
#accessing or modifying attributes directly
```

```python
class Animal:
    def __init__(self, name, sound):
        self.name = name
        self.sound = sound

#instantiating object
animal = Animal('Dog', 'bark')

#accessing attributes
print(animal.name)
print(animal.sound)

#modifying attributes
animal.name = 'Elephant'
animal.sound = 'snort'

#accessing attributes
print(animal.name)
print(animal.sound)
print(animal.name)
print(animal.sound)
```

Output:
Dog
bark

Instead of directly accessing or modifying the attributes of a class through its instances, you have the option to use getter and setter methods.

Getter and setter methods

Getter methods are used to retrieve the values of attributes, while setter methods are used to modify or update the values of attributes. By using getter and setter methods, you can enforce additional logic or validation before accessing or modifying the attributes.

Here's an example of how getter and setter methods can be implemented for the Animal class:

```python
class Animal:
    def __init__(self, name, sound):
```

```python
        self.name = name
        self.sound = sound

    def get_name(self):
        #getter method for name attribute
        return self.name

    def set_name(self, name):
        #setter method for name attribute
        print(f'setting name to {name}')
        self.name = name

    def get_sound(self):
        #getter method for sound attribute
        return self.sound

    def set_sound(self, sound):
        #setter method for sound attribute
        print(f'setting sound to {sound}')
        self.sound = sound

animal = Animal('Dog', 'bark')

print(animal.get_name())
print(animal.get_sound())

animal.set_name('Elephant')
animal.set_sound('snort')

print(animal.get_name())
print(animal.get_sound())
```

Output:
Dog
bark
setting name to Elephant
setting sound to snort

In this modified code, getter methods (get_name(), get_sound()) are used to access the attribute values, and setter methods (set_name(), set_sound()) are used to modify the attribute values.

Pro Tip:

It is generally not considered a good practice to create separate getter and setter methods for class attributes. Instead, a better and cleaner approach is to use properties.

Properties in Python

Properties are like a set of rules that determine how you can access, modify, or remove attributes. They allow you to encapsulate data within a class and define custom behaviour for attribute operations.

Instead of cluttering your codes with the getters and setters, you can implement properties using the built-in property method. This allows you to define getter, setter, and deleter methods for an attribute, giving you control over how the attribute is accessed, modified, or removed.

Property is an in-built function that allows you to turn an attribute of a class into properties or managed attributes.

To create a property, you can use the property function and provide it with the appropriate arguments.

Here is the definition of the property() function:

Property (fget=None, fset=None, fdel=None, doc=None)

- **fget (optional):** This is a function that returns the value of the managed attribute. When you access the property, this function will be called to retrieve the value. If fget is not provided, the property will be read-only.
- **fset (optional):** This is a function that allows you to change the value of the managed attribute. When you assign a value to the property, this function will be called to set the new value. If fset is not provided, the property will be read-only.
- **fdel (optional):** This allows you to delete the managed attribute. When you use the del statement on the property, this function will be called to perform any necessary cleanup or deletion operations.
- **doc (optional):** This is a string representing the docstring (documentation) of the property. This can be used to provide information about the property to users of the class.

At a minimum, you should provide a setter function (fset) if you want to allow assignment to the property.

Now, let's modify the previous example to use the property method.

```python
class Animal:
    def __init__(self, name, sound):
        self._name = name
        self._sound = sound

    def _get_name(self):
        print(f'accessing name: {self._name}')
        return self._name

    def _set_name(self, value):
        print(f'setting name to: {self._name}')
        self._name = value
    def _get_sound(self):
        print(f'accessing sound: {self._sound}')
        return self._sound

    def _set_sound(self, value):
        print(f'setting sound to: {self._sound}')
        self._sound = value

    name = property(fget=_get_name, fset=_set_name, fdel=None,
doc='name of animal')
    sound = property(fget=_get_sound, fset=_set_sound, fdel=None,
doc='sound of animal')

animal = Animal('Dog', 'bark')
print(animal.name)
print(animal.sound)

animal.name = 'Elephant'
animal.sound = 'snort'

print(animal.name)
print(animal.sound)
```

Output:
accessing name: Dog
Dog

accessing sound: bark
bark
setting name to: Dog
setting sound to: bark
accessing name: Elephant
Elephant
accessing sound: snort
Snort

Also, properties allow you to expose attributes as part of public interface. This means that if you need to change the underlying implementation of an interface, you can turn the interface into a property any time.

Since Python does not have private, protected and public access modifiers like in java or c#, you can achieve something close to private and public modifiers by preceding an underscore before an identifier to indicate private and not including it to indicate public.

Names starting with a leading underscore in the above code are considered as private, while those without leading underscores are public.

Using property as a decorator

A decorator is a function that accepts another function as argument and returns another function.

Now, imagine you have some functionalities or tasks that you want to apply to multiple functions in your program. Instead of copying and pasting those functionalities into each function, decorators provide a more elegant solution.

You can define a decorator function that encapsulates those functionalities, and then apply the decorator to other functions.

To apply a decorator to a function, you can use a special syntax called the "decorator syntax." This involves placing the @ symbol before the name of the decorator function, right above the function you want to decorate.

```
def decorator_func(func):
    result = f'Output: {func()}'
    return result
@decorator_func
```

```
def func():
    return 'this is a function'

my_func = func
print(my_func)
```

Output:

this is a function

> **Pro Tip:**
> *This is a shorthand way of saying func = decorator_func(func).*

```
def func():
    return 'this is a function'

my_func = decorator_func(func)
print(my_func)
```

This means that the decorator_func will be applied to func before func is defined, and if you run the program, you will get a similar output:

Output:

this is a function

Property decorator

The property decorator is used to customize the behaviour of attribute access operations, such as getting, setting, and deleting a value. It allows you to define special methods that are automatically called when these operations are performed on an object's attribute and these methods include the following:

Getter Method: To define a property and customize how the attribute is accessed, you decorate a method with @property. This method is called the getter method and is responsible for returning the attribute value. Any docstring you want to include for the property should be placed in this getter method.

Setter Method: If you want to customize how the attribute is set, you use @attr.setter decorator. Here, attr refers to the name of the property you defined using the @property decorator. The setter method is responsible for assigning a new value to the attribute.

Deleter Method: If you want to customize how the attribute is deleted, you use @attr.deleter decorator. Again, attr is the name of the property you defined using @property. The deleter method is responsible for removing the attribute.

Here's an example to help illustrate the concept:

```python
class Animal:
    def __init__(self, name, sound):
        self._name = name
        self._sound = sound

    @property
    def name(self):
        print(f'accessing name: {self._name}')
        return self._name

    @name.setter
    def name(self, value):
        print(f'setting name to: {self._name}')
        self._name = value

    @property
    def sound(self):
        print(f'accessing sound: {self._sound}')
        return self._sound

    @sound.setter
    def sound(self, value):
        print(f'setting sound to: {self._sound}')
        self._sound = value


animal = Animal('Dog', 'bark')
print(animal.name)
print(animal.sound)

animal.name = 'Elephant'
animal.sound = 'snort'

print(animal.name)
```

```
print(animal.sound)
```

If you run this code, you will get the same output as the previous one.

accessing name: Dog
Dog
accessing sound: bark
bark
setting name to: Dog
setting sound to: bark
accessing name: Elephant
Elephant
accessing sound: snort
Snort

You can use the property to make an attribute read only by only decorating the getter method and not specifying the setter method.

```python
class Animal:
    def __init__(self, name, sound):
        self._name = name
        self._sound = sound

    @property
    def name(self):
        print(f'accessing name: {self._name}')
        return self._name

    @property
    def sound(self):
        print(f'accessing sound: {self._sound}')
        return self._sound


animal = Animal('Dog', 'bark')
print(animal.name)
print(animal.sound)
animal.name = 'Elephant'
animal.sound = 'snort'
```

Read-only and write-only decorator properties

When you define a property without a setter method, it becomes read-only, meaning you cannot directly modify its value. If you try to assign a new value to a read-only attribute, it will result in an AttributeError. This error occurs when you attempt to change the value of an attribute that is not allowed to be modified directly.

On the other hand, if you want to create a write-only attribute, you can define a property where the getter method raises an exception. This means that you can assign a value to the attribute, but you won't be able to access its value. If you try to access a write-only attribute, it will raise an exception and prevent you from retrieving its value.

Take a look at this example:

```python
class Animal:
    def __init__(self, name, sound):
        self._name = name
        self._sound = sound

    @property
    def name(self):
        raise AttributeError('Access denied!')

    @name.setter
    def name(self, value):
        print(f'setting name to: {self._name}')
        self._name = value

    @property
    def sound(self):
        raise AttributeError('Access denied!')

    @sound.setter
    def sound(self, value):
        print(f'setting sound to: {self._sound}')
        self._sound = value

animal = Animal('Dog', 'bark')
print(animal.name)
print(animal.sound)
```

```
animal.name = 'Elephant'
animal.sound = 'snort'
```

In this example, the attributes "name" and "sound " are defined as write-only attributes. This means that you can assign new values to these attributes, but you cannot directly access their values.

The getter methods of the name and sound attributes raise an AttributeError with the message 'Access denied!' when you try to access them. This serves as a way to deny direct access to these attributes and ensure that they cannot be retrieved without proper authorization.

Validating user inputs

A typical application of properties is the validating user inputs. Validation is a great way to ensure that the data entered by users meets certain criteria or constraints. Here's how it works:

You can use the @property decorator to define a property for an attribute. By combining this decorator with a setter method, you can perform validations on inputs.

Let's say we have a class called "User " with an attribute called "username ". You want to validate that the name provided by the username meets certain requirements, such as being at least 3 characters long.

```
#validations

class User:
    def __init__(self):
        self._username = ""

    @property
    def username(self):
        return self._username

    @username.setter
    def username(self, value):
        if len(value) >= 3:
            self._username = value
```

```
        else:
            raise ValueError("name must be at least 4 characters
long.")

user = User()
user.username = 'adams'
print(user.username)
user.username = 'ad'
```

Now, whenever a user tries to assign a value to username, the setter method is automatically called. The validation is performed, and if the input meets the criteria, the value is stored. If the input is invalid, an exception is raised.

Using properties for validating user inputs allows you to control the validity of the data and provide meaningful feedback to the user if the input doesn't meet the required criteria.

However, it is recommended that you use properties selectively and only when there is a specific requirement for additional processing or validation. For simple attributes that don't require any extra processing, it's generally better to use regular attributes without properties. This keeps the code simpler, improves performance, and makes it easier to maintain.

Descriptors

Properties and descriptors are two mechanisms in Python that allow you to control how attributes are accessed and provide additional custom behavior.

Properties allow you to determine how attributes are accessed or modified. By using properties, you can define custom logic that determines what happens when an attribute is accessed, set, or deleted. In other words, properties allow you to add extra functionality to attribute access.

On the other hand, descriptors provide a flexible and reusable way to define custom behaviour that can be applied to multiple attributes across different classes.

They allow you to define special methods that are called automatically when certain attribute operations are performed, such as getting, setting, or deleting an attribute.

To use descriptors, you need to create a descriptor class and connect it to a specific attribute in another class. This is achieved by assigning an instance of the descriptor class to a variable within the class that will utilize it.

By connecting the descriptor class to an attribute, you can control how that attribute behaves when it is accessed, modified, or removed. This gives you more flexibility and control over how your objects interact with their attributes, allowing you to add custom logic or validation to attribute operations.

Consider this example:

```python
class Movement:
    def __get__(self, instance, owner=None):
        return 'moves'
class Animal:
    movement = Movement()

    def __init__(self, name):
        self.name = name
```

In this example, the Movement descriptor is used in the Animal class. Inside the Animal class, there is an attribute called "movement," and it is set as an instance of the Movement class.

By assigning an instance of the Movement class to a class variable called "movement" within the Animal class, you indicate that the movement attribute of the Animal class should be managed by the Movement Descriptor.

This means that whenever you access or modify the movement attribute on an instance of the Animal class, the descriptor's methods will be invoked.

```python
animal = Animal('Fish')
print(animal.movement)
```

When you try to access the animal.movement attribute, the descriptor's __get__ method is automatically called. In this case, the __get__ method simply returns the string 'moves'.

Output:

Moves

Descriptor methods

When you assign a class variable to a descriptor, you associate its behaviour with a specific attribute of the class.

By using descriptors and associating them with class variables, you have the ability to customize the behaviour of specific attributes in your class, controlling how they are accessed, assigned, and deleted.

Descriptor methods are typically implemented using the descriptor protocol, which involves defining one or more of the following special methods in a class:

1. __get__(self, instance, owner): This method is called when you access the attribute's value and can return a different value than the original attribute value.
2. __set__(self, instance, value): This method is called when assigning a value to an attribute.
3. __delete__(self, instance): This method is called when deleting an attribute from an instance.

Here, "self " represents the descriptor instance, "instance " represents the class instance involved in the attribute access or assignment, "owner " represents the owning class of the descriptor, and value refers to the value being assigned to the attribute.

By implementing these methods in a class, you can control how attribute access is handled.

For example, when the movement attribute is accessed on an instance of the Animal class, the __get__ method of the Movement descriptor is called, which causes it to return the value "moves".

Dynamic Attribute Retrieval

Instead of just getting a fixed value for an attribute, descriptors enable you to fetch the value dynamically based on what's happening in your code at runtime. You can use descriptors to figure out what value to return for an attribute or do some extra processing before returning it.

In the case of the Animal class, you can modify the Movement descriptor to determine the movement of an instance of the Animal on the name.

Here's the modified version of the code:

```
class Movement:
    def __get__(self, instance, owner=None):
        moves = {'Bird':'flies', 'Fish':'swims', 'Dog': 'walks or
runs'}
        if instance.name in moves:
            return moves[instance.name]
        return 'moves'

class Animal:
    movement = Movement()

    def __init__(self, name):
        self.name = name

animal = Animal('Dog')
print(animal.movement)
```

Now, the movement of an animal is determined based on the name provided when creating an instance of the Animal class.

If the name matches one of the animals in the predefined dictionary, the corresponding movement is returned. However, if the name does not match any animal in the dictionary, a default value of 'moves' is returned.

```
animal = Animal('Human')
print(animal.movement)
```

Output:
walks or runs
moves

Implementing validation logic

Descriptors allows you to enforce validations on attribute values, ensuring that they meet certain criteria or constraints before being assigned to an attribute. To use descriptors for validations, you can implement validation logic within the descriptor's __set__ method.

Now, let's improve the Animal class to implement validations using the Movement descriptor.

```
#validating names using set

class Movement:
    def __get__(self, instance, owner=None):
        moves = {'Bird':'flies', 'Fish':'swims', 'Dog': 'walks or
runs'}
        return moves[instance.name]

    def __set__(self, instance, value):
        if instance.name not in moves:
            raise ValueError('Incorrect name of animal')
        instance.name = value

class Animal:
    movement = Movement()

    def __init__(self, name):
        self.name = name

animal = Animal('Bird')
print(animal.movement)
```

In this example, since the name attribute is "Bird," the movement attribute is "flies" according to the moves dictionary. If you access animal.movement, it returns "flies" as expected.

However, if you were to provide an incorrect animal name during initialization, like 'Lion', the __set__ method would raise a ValueError with the message "Incorrect name of animal."

Getting, setting and deleting attributes

Before concluding this chapter, let's write a program that uses the functionality of the __get__, __set__, and __delete__ methods within the descriptor.

```
class Name:

    def __get__(self, instance, owner=None):
        print(f'accessing {instance._name}')
        return instance._name.upper()

    def __set__(self, instance, value):
        print(f'updating {instance._name} to {value}')
        instance._name = value

    def __delete__(self, instance):
        del instance._name
        print('deleting...')

class Animal:
    name = Name()
    def __init__(self, name):
        self._name = name
```

The example above defines a descriptor class called Name that handles attribute access, assignment, and deletion for the name attribute in the Animal class.

The __get__ method prints a message and returns the uppercase version of the _name attribute when the name attribute is accessed. The __set__ method updates the _name attribute and prints a message when a value is assigned to the name attribute. The __delete__ method deletes the _name attribute and prints a message when the name attribute is deleted.

```
animal = Animal('Bird')
print(animal.name)
animal.name = 'Dog'
animal.name = 'Fish'
print(animal.name)
del animal.name
```

If you run the code, you will get the following outputs:

accessing Bird

BIRD
updating Bird to Dog
updating Dog to Fish
accessing Fish
FISH
deleting...

Summary

In this chapter, you learnt how to use properties and descriptors for controlled attribute access, validation, and manipulation. You learnt how to use properties to define special methods or manage the behaviour of attributes and descriptors to have control over attribute access, modification, and deletion.

Practice Exercises

1. What is a property?
2. What are the advantages of using properties?
3. What are decorators and how are they used?
4. What is the difference between properties and attributes?
5. How do you implement properties with decorators?
6. What are the use cases for decorators?
7. Write a program using a decorator to find how times a function have been executed.
8. What are the limitations for using decorators?
9. Write a program that uses decorators to format phone numbers

EXPLORING THE POWER OF DATA SCIENCE

"The greatest obstacle to discovery is not ignorance - it is the illusion of knowledge."
- Daniel J. Boorstin

No doubt, data itself is valuable, but extracting actionable information from it is where the real power lies. It can be quite challenging, especially when dealing with large amounts of data. The sheer volume of data can make it overwhelming to extract useful insights. However, those who can successfully do so gain a significant advantage over their competitors. In today's world, data has revolutionized the way we make decisions by allowing us to uncover patterns, trends, and correlations that may not be apparent at first glance. Hence, allowing us to make informed predictions, optimize processes, and make data-driven strategies.

Learning outcome

In this chapter, you will learn:
- Basics of data science.
- To utilize the NumPy and Pandas libraries for data manipulation and analysis.
- To visualize data using Matplotlib.

Data Analysis with Python

Data science is one of the fastest-growing fields, with a rapidly increasing demand for skilled professionals. Just think about social media, online shopping, and all the other things people do online.

All of this creates a massive amount of data, which contain valuable information that can help businesses and organizations understand customer behaviour, predict trends, improve products and services, and optimize business processes.

By leveraging the power of data, they can figure out what customers like best, spot trends in the market, and make really smart decisions based on data. This helps them serve their customers better and stay ahead of their competitors.

Basically, data science is about using data to learn new things, make predictions, and solve problems. It combines different disciplines such as statistics, mathematics, computer science, and domain knowledge to analyze large amounts of data and extract meaningful information from it.

Data scientists collect data from surveys, experiments, and databases. They use statistical methods and machine learning algorithms to find valuable insights in the data. Then, they present this information visually through charts, graphs, or maps.

Interestingly, Python has emerged as a preferred programming language by many developers for data analysis with several libraries like NumPy, Pandas, and Matplotlib that make the task of data analysis an easy one.

Understanding NumPy

NumPy is a Python library with a powerful set of tools and functions that allow users to work with numerical data efficiently and effectively. It is widely used together with Pandas, Matplotlib and many other data science and scientific python packages.

The strength of NumPy lies in its ability to perform operations on arrays efficiently and quickly. The core of NumPy operations is based on a special array type known as ndarray or n-dimensional array.

This specialized array type allows for quick and efficient execution of mathematical operations on arrays, including addition, subtraction, multiplication, and more, with great efficiency, even on large datasets.

Unlike regular Python lists, NumPy arrays are designed for numerical computations and provide much better performance.

Types of arrays

There are basically three types of arrays in NumPy and they include the following:

- Dimensional
- 2-Dimensional
- Multidimensional

1-Dimensional Array

1-dimension arrays, also known as vectors are used to represent a sequence of elements that are arranged in a single row. You can think of it as a line of boxes, where each box holds a value or an element.

These elements are arranged in a single row, one after another. It's like having a sequence of data elements neatly lined up in a straight line.

2-Dimensional Array

2-dimensional array, also known as matrix is used to represent a grid of elements that are organized in rows and columns. You can think of it like a big box filled with small boxes. Each small box holds a value or a piece of data. These small boxes are arranged in rows, like the rows of a table, and each row has its own set of boxes.

Two-dimensional arrays are really useful when you need to organize data in a tabular format or perform various calculations that involve rows and columns.

Multidimensional Array

A multidimensional array is an array that has more than two dimensions. They are also called n-dimensional arrays, where "n" represents the number of dimensions.

For instance, a three-dimensional array presents a collection of elements arranged in three dimensions. It is like having a cube with rows, columns, and depth.

You can think of it as a big cube composed of individual cube cells with each containing a specific value. This cube is structured into layers, much like stacking multiple two-dimensional arrays on top of each other.

> **Pro Tip:**
> *A special type of multidimensional array, known as a tensor, specifically refers to a three-dimensional array.*

Installing NumPy

In order to use the functionalities provided by NumPy in your programs, you need to have it installed. Using the pip, you can install NumPy by typing the following command in your terminal and hitting the enter key:

```
Pip install numpy
```

On a successful installation, you can access all the functionalities that comes with the library.

But then, you still need to import the library into your program or scripts to use it.

```
import numpy
```

> **Pro Tip:**
> *While you can directly use import numpy to access NumPy's functionalities, it is common practice to import numpy with an alias, often referred to as "np."*

By using the alias "np," you can access NumPy's functionalities using the shorter prefix "np" instead of typing "numpy" every time.

How to create a basic array

You can create an array using the np.array() function. This function requires that you provide a sequence of items, which can be a list or a tuple.

For example, you can create a basic array with the Numpy from a list by passing a list as an argument to np.array() function.

```
num = [1, 2, 3, 4, 5]
num_array = np.array(num)

print(num_array)
```

If you print this array, you will get the following output:

[1 2 3 4 5]

You can also create arrays using the linspace() and the arrange() functions of the Numpy.

The linspace() function

This function allows you to create a list with numbers that are evenly distributed between a starting value and an ending value.

For instance, you may want to create an array starting with the number 1 and ending at 5. Instead of listing out all the numbers one by one, you can simply the starting number, the ending number and the number of equally spaced points between them, as input to this function. It will then generate all the numbers automatically, evenly filling the gap between the start and end values.

The syntax is:

np.linspace(start, end, points)

The "start " and the "end " are the starting and ending values of the sequence, while "points" is the number of equally spaced points you want to generate between the start and end values

```
num_array = np.linspace(1, 5, 5)
print(num_array)
```

Output:
[1. 2. 3. 4. 5.]

This function is particularly useful when you need a specific number of evenly spaced values within a given range, such as when plotting graphs or performing numerical computations.

The arange() function

The arange() function is used to generate a sequence of numbers within a specified range. This function requires that you the starting and ending values.

For example, if you want to create a sequence of numbers from 1 to 10. You can use the arange() function, setting 1 as the starting value and 10 as the ending value.

```
num_array = np.arange(1,10)
print(num_array)
```

Output:
[1 2 3 4 5 6 7 8 9]

However, you can specify the step or interval between numbers by using a third argument. The default value of the step is 1, and if you don't include it, the numbers will be increasing by 1.

```
num_array = np.arange(1,10,2)
print(num_array)

num_array = np.arange(1,10,3)
print(num_array)
```

Output:
[1 3 5 7 9]
[1 4 7]

Data types in numpy

NumPy provides a wide range of data types that can be used to define the elements of an array. These data types determine the size in memory and the precision of the values stored in the array.

The following are some commonly used data types in NumPy:

Integer Types
int8, int16, int32, int64: Signed integers with different bit sizes.
uint8, uint16, uint32, uint64: Unsigned integers with different bit sizes.

Floating-Point Types
float16, float32, float64: Floating-point numbers with different levels of precision.
float128: Extended-precision floating-point number.
half, single, double: Aliases for float16, float32, and float64, respectively.

Boolean Type
bool: Boolean data type representing True or False values.

String Types
str_, unicode_: String types to store text data.
bytes_: Byte string type to store binary data.

> **Pro Tip:**
> *You can create a NumPy array with a specific data type, by assigning the value to the dtype keyword argument of the np.array() function.*

```
num = [1, 2, 3, 4, 5]
num_array = np.array(num, dtype=np.float32)
print(num_array)

num_array = np.array(num, dtype=np.int32)
print(num_array)
```

Output:
[1. 2. 3. 4. 5.]
[1 2 3 4 5]

Attributes of an array

Attributes are properties or characteristics of an array that provides useful information about the array itself, rather than specific data elements within the array. They provide essential information about the array, such as its shape, size, data type, and more.

With this information, you can effectively manipulate and analyze the data stored in the array.

You can access these attributes using the dot notation by appending the desired attribute name to your NumPy array object.

Shape

The shape of a NumPy array refers to the number of elements along each axis. For example, the shape of a 1-dimensional array is the number of elements contained in the array. For a 2-dimensional array, the shape is represented by a tuple indicating the number of elements in each row and each column, respectively.

```
num = [1,2,3,4,5,6,7,8,9]
num_array = np.array(num)
print(num_array.shape)

num = [[1,2,3], [4,5,6], [7,8,9]]
num_array = np.array(num)
print(num_array.shape)
```

Output:
(9,)
(3, 3)

Dimension

The dimension of an array indicates the different axes or directions along which the array spreads. Each dimension corresponds to a specific axis, and the number of elements along each axis defines the size of that particular dimension.

To obtain the dimension of an array, you can use the ndarray.ndim attribute. This attribute provides a single integer value that reveals the total number of dimensions present in the array.

For a one-dimensional array, the ndim attribute will be 1 and for a two-dimensional array, the ndim attribute will be 2.

```
num = [1,2,3,4,5,6,7,8,9]
num_array = np.array(num)
print(num_array.ndim)

num = [[1,2,3], [4,5,6], [7,8,9]]
num_array = np.array(num)
print(num_array.ndim)
```

Output:
1
2

Size

This attribute represents the total number of elements in an array. By using the ndarry.size, you can get the size of an array.

This attribute returns a single integer value representing the count of all elements present in the array, regardless of its shape or dimensions.

```
num = [1,2,3,4,5,6,7,8,9]
```

```
num_array = np.array(num)
print(num_array.size)

num = [[1,2,3], [4,5,6], [7,8,9]]
num_array = np.array(num)
print(num_array.size)
```

Output:
9
9

Type

This provides information about the data type of the elements in a NumPy array and can be accessed using the dtype attribute of the array. When you access the type attribute, it gives you a single value indicating the specific data type of all the elements within that array.

Of course, different data types require different amounts of memory, and they have different capabilities for handling mathematical operations. Therefore, knowing the data type helps you work with the array efficiently.

```
num = [1,2,3,4,5,6,7,8,9]
num_array = np.array(num)
print(num_array.dtype)
```

Output:
int64

Accessing arrays

The interesting thing about NumPy arrays is the ability to access and manipulate arrays with ease. There are various techniques for accessing arrays in NumPy but in this book, we will be looking at indexing, slicing and boolean indexing. By using these techniques, you can access specific elements or extract portions of a NumPy array.

Indexing

Just like you can access individual elements in a Python list using their positions (index), you can do the same with NumPy arrays. The first element in an array has an index of 0, the second element has an index of 1, and so on. By specifying the index of the element you want, you can fetch that particular number from the array.

In a one-dimensional array, the elements are organized in a single row or column. To access a specific element within this array, you provide the index of the element.

```
num = [1,2,3,4,5]
num_array = np.array(num)
print(num_array[0])
print(num_array[1])
print(num_array[2])
```

Output:
1
2
3

However, for 2-dimensional array, elements are organized in a grid with rows and columns. To access a specific element within this array, you use indexing with two values. The first value represents the row, while the second value represents the column.

```
num = [[1,2,3], [4,5,6], [7,8,9]]
num_array = np.array(num)
print(num_array[0, 0])
print(num_array[0, 1])
print(num_array[0, 2])
```

Output:
1
2
3

Slicing Arrays

Slicing is a way to extract a range of specific elements of the NumPy array. It allows you to extract one or more elements from the array rather than just one. To slice an array, you are required to provide a starting index and an ending index.

```
num = [1,2,3,4,5]
num_array = np.array(num)
print(num_array[0:3])
print(num_array[3:5])
```

Output:
[1 2 3]
[4 5]

Boolean Indexing

Boolean indexing allows you to access the elements in an array based on some condition. This involves the use of a Boolean (True or False) condition inside square brackets [] to select only the elements that satisfy the condition.

By using the Boolean condition inside square brackets with the array, you create a new array containing only the elements that meet the condition.

```
num = [1,2,3,4,5]
num_array = np.array(num)
print(num_array[num_array > 2])
print(num_array[num_array < 5])
print(num_array[num_array % 2 == 0])
```

Output:
[3 4 5]
[1 2 3 4]
[2 4]

Adding and removing

NumPy provides various functions that allow you to interactively add or remove items from the array. This means you can dynamically modify the content of the array by adding new elements or removing existing elements.

Adding Elements

Numpy provides various functions that allow you to add elements at the end of an already existing array or to a specific location within the array. To add an element to the end of an array, you use the append() function and to add an element to a specific position in an array, you use the insert() function.

np.append() function

This function allows you to add elements at the end of the array. In other words, you can use the np.append() function to extend an array by appending new elements to the last positions.

```
num = [1,2,3,4,5]
num_array = np.array(num)
print(num_array)
num_array = np.append(num_array, 6)
print(num_array)
```

Output:
[1 2 3 4 5 6]

np.insert() function

This function allows you to add elements at specific positions within the array. It allows you to choose where you want to insert new elements. To use np.insert(), you need to provide the array, the index position where you want to insert, and the new element(s) you wish to add.

```
num = [1,2,3,4,5]
num_array = np.array(num)
print(num_array)
num_array = np.insert(num_array, 0, 0)
print(num_array)
num_array = np.insert(num_array, 2, 99)
print(num_array)
```

Output:
[1 2 3 4 5]
[0 1 2 3 4 5]
[0 1 99 2 3 4 5]

Removing Elements

NumPy allows you to not only add elements but also remove elements from an array. You can use the numpy.delete() function to remove elements from an array along a specified axis by specifying the array and the indices of the elements you want to remove.

```
num = [1,2,3,4,5]
num_array = np.array(num)
print(num_array)
num_array = np.delete(num_array, 0)
print(num_array)

num_array = np.delete(num_array, 3)
print(num_array)
```

Output:
[2 3 4 5]
[2 3 4]

Sorting arrays

Sorting is the process of arranging the elements of an array in a specific order. Typically, it is usually in ascending or descending order. The essence of sorting is to organize the elements in a way that makes it easier to search for specific values, perform certain computations, or simply present the data in a more meaningful manner.

You can sort an array by using the np.sort() function of the NumPy or the ndarray.sort() function.

Sorting with np.sort()

The np.sort() function is used to sort the elements of an array in ascending order along a specified axis. To use this function, you are required to provide the array to be sorted as an argument to this function and it returns asorted array.

```
num = [5,3,1,4,2]
num_array = np.array(num)
result = np.sort(num_array)
print(result)
```

Output:
[1 2 3 4 5]

However, you must keep in mind that this function sorts an array without changing the original array. So, if you print out the original array, you will discover that it is unchanged.

```
print(num_array)
```

Output:
[5 3 1 4 2]

Sorting with ndarray.sort()

You can also perform sorting operation on arrays using ndarray.sort() function. However, unlike the np.sort(), where a new sorted array is returned, leaving the original array unchanged, ndarray.sort() directly modifies the array. It performs an in-place sorting of the elements, meaning it modifies the original array.

```
num_array.sort()
print(num_array)
```

Output:
[1 2 3 4 5]

Mathematical operations on arrays

You can perform arithmetic operations on arrays element-by-element. This means you can add, subtract, multiply, divide, raise to a power, and perform other mathematical operations on corresponding elements of arrays, making it easy to carry out calculations across multiple data points efficiently and conveniently.

```
num_array1 = np.array([1, 2, 3])
num_array2 = np.array([4, 5, 6])

#addition
result = num_array1 + num_array2
print(result)
```

```
#subtraction
result = num_array1 - num_array2
print(result)

#multiplication
result = num_array1 * num_array2
print(result)

#division
result = num_array1 / num_array2
print(result)
```

Output:
[5 7 9]
[-3 -3 -3]
[4 10 18]
[0.25 0.4 0.5]

Also, NumPy offers a diverse range of built-in mathematical functions that allows you to apply mathematical operations to the elements of arrays. These functions encompass a variety of operations such as exponentiation, logarithm, square root, absolute value, trigonometric functions, statistical functions, and many others.

By using these functions, you can perform complex mathematical computations with ease and efficiency.

```
num = [1,2,3,4,5,6,7,8,9,10]
num_array = np.array(num)

#square root
squared_array = np.sqrt(num_array)
print(squared_array)

#mean
mean = np.mean(num_array)
print(mean)

#median
median = np.median(num_array)
print(median)
```

```
#standard deviation
std_dev = np.std(num_array)
print(std_dev)
```

Output:
[1.   1.41421356 1.73205081 2.   2.23606798 2.44948974
 2.64575131 2.82842712 3.   3.16227766]
5.5
5.5
2.8722813232690143

Generating random numbers

Generating random numbers is fundamental in so many aspects of research and analysis. Whether it's simulating real-world scenarios, testing algorithms, or conducting statistical analysis, having reliable random numbers is important.

NumPy provides a robust module called "random" and this module comes with a variety of functions for generating random data. With this module, you can easily create random numbers that can be used in various situations.

Generating Random Integers

When it comes to generating random integers, you can use the random.randint() function of the random module. This function allows you to generate random integer numbers within a specific range.

To use this function, you are required to provide the lowest number that you want to include, otherwise known as lower bound, and the highest number you want to exclude, otherwise known as the upper bound.

The following example uses this function to generate numbers between 1 and 10, but excluding 10.

```
rand_num = np.random.randint(1,10)
print(rand_num)
```

Creating Random Arrays

Apart from just generating random numbers, you can take it a step further and create entire arrays filled with random numbers as well. You can use the random.rand() function to generate arrays with random numbers ranging from 0 to 1.

To use this function, you are required to provide the desired number of rows and columns as arguments.

```
rand_array = np.random.rand(5)
print(rand_array)

rand_array = np.random.rand(2,4)
print(rand_array)
```

Output:
[0.97952541 0.98972613 0.93062452 0.07695195 0.02192153]
[[0.41545466 0.98138275 0.98030105 0.7093207]
[0.15885744 0.62088258 0.11549422 0.12478255]]

Setting the Random Seed

While generating random numbers, there are instances where achieving reproducible and consistent results becomes crucial. To achieve this, you must set a random seed.

> **Pro Tip:**
> *When you set a random seed, it initializes the internal state of the random number generator, ensuring that the sequence of random numbers generated is reproducible.*

By setting a random seed, you guarantee that the same sequence of random numbers is generated each time your code runs, as long as you use the same seed value.

However, it is essential to set the seed before generating the array to ensure that you consistently obtain the exact same array whenever you execute your code.

```
np.random.seed(12)
rand_array = np.random.rand(5)
```

```
print(rand_array)
```

Broadcasting

Typically, for mathematical operations involving arrays, it's necessary for the arrays to share the same shape, implying an equal number of elements in each dimension.

However, broadcasting in NumPy introduces a smart solution. It allows NumPy to handle operations between arrays with different shapes by automatically adjusting the dimensions of the smaller array (or even a scalar) to align with the shape of the larger array.

This adjustment is done in a way that enables element-wise operations to be performed without explicitly creating larger arrays.

By performing broadcasting, NumPy can carry out element-wise operations efficiently, even when the arrays have different shapes.

Let's take a look at some examples:

```
num_array1 = np.array([1, 2])
num_array2 = np.array([[10, 20], [30, 40]])
result = num_array1 + num_array2
print(result)

num_array3 = np.array([10, 20, 30])
num_array4 = np.array([[[1], [2]], [[3], [4]]])
result = num_array3 + num_array4
print(result)
```

In the above example, the 1-Dimensional array num_array1 is broadcasted along the rows of num_array2, allowing the addition operation to be performed element-wise. Also, the 1-Dimensional array num_array3 is broadcasted along both the rows and columns of each 2D subarray in num_array4, allowing the addition operation to be performed element-wise across the entire 3D array.

Outputs:
[[11 22]

[31 42]]

[[[11 21 31]
[12 22 32]]
[[13 23 33]
[14 24 34]]]

Nevertheless, it's essential to note that broadcasting is not feasible when the arrays possess differing numbers of dimensions, and neither array has a dimension with a size of 1 that can be expanded to align with the other. Consequently, attempting a broadcasting operation in such cases will result in a ValueError.

Reshaping a NumPy array

Reshaping refers to the process of modifying the shape of a NumPy array without altering its data. It enables you to convert arrays between one-dimensional, two-dimensional, and higher-dimensional structures, as well as changing the number of elements in each dimension.

NumPy provides the reshape() function, which serves as the primary tool for reshaping arrays. This function allows you to specify the desired new shape for the array as a tuple of dimensions.

However, the total number of elements in the original array must match the total number of elements in the reshaped array, otherwise you will get a ValueError.

```
num_array = np.array([[1, 2, 3], [4, 5, 6], [7,8,9], [10,11,12]])
rsh_array = np.reshape(num_array, (3,4))
print(rsh_array)
```

Output:
[[1 2 3 4]
 [5 6 7 8]
 [9 10 11 12]]

However, to reshape a 2-dimensional array to a 1-dimensional array, you have to use the np.ndarray.flatten method or the np.ravel method. Both of these methods will convert the 2D array into a 1D array by flattening the elements row-wise.

```
num_array = np.array([[1, 2, 3], [4, 5, 6], [7,8,9], [10,11,12]])
result = num_array.flatten()
print(result)
result = np.ravel(num_array)
print(result)
```

Output:
[1 2 3 4 5 6 7 8 9 10 11 12]
[1 2 3 4 5 6 7 8 9 10 11 12]

Data Manipulation with Pandas

Pandas is an open-source Python library designed to handle and manipulate data in a flexible and intuitive manner. It is built on top of Numpy, which makes it highly optimized for efficient data processing and analysis.

Pandas provides numerous functions that simplify data manipulation, exploration, and analysis, making it an essential tool for data science. It allows you to filter, select, sort, group, reshape, and aggregate data in a flexible manner. Also, it provides you with a wide range of functions for data analysis, including descriptive statistics, data aggregation, grouping, and merging.

Pandas seamlessly integrates with other popular data science libraries, such as Numpy and Matplotlib.

Installing pandas

You can use the pip to install pandas by typing the following command in your terminal.

```
pip install pandas
```

Like every other third-party library, you are required to import it into your program to be able to use it.

```
import pandas
```

However, it is a common convention to import it using the alias "pd". This alias is chosen to make the code more concise and readable.

Instead of typing "pandas" every time you want to use a Pandas function or class, you can simply use the shorter "pd" alias.

Creating data

There are two primary data structures in Pandas and they include the following:

- Series
- DataFrame

Series

A Series is one of the fundamental building blocks of pandas. It a one-dimensional array-like object that can hold data of various types, such as integers, floats, strings and Python objects.

You can create a Series from various data sources including lists, NumPy arrays, dictionaries, and more.

By using the pd.Series() constructor, you can create a series by passing the data as an argument.

Now, let's create a series using the Python list as a data source.

```
data = [1,2,3,4,5]

series = pd.Series(data)
print(series)
```

Output:
```
0   1
1   2
2   3
3   4
4   5
dtype: int64
```

Also, you can create a Series with custom labels or index by passing a list of data along with a list of labels to the pd.Series() constructor. You can as well assign name to a series.

```
data = [1,2,3,4,5]
series = pd.Series(data, index=['A', 'B', 'C', 'D', 'E'],
name='Numbers')
print(series)
```

Output:
A 1
B 2
C 3
D 4
E 5
Name: Numbers, dtype: int64

The output shows the contents of the Series series, where each value is associated with its custom index label. Additionally, the name of the Series ('Numbers') is displayed, and the data type of the Series elements is 'int64', indicating integer values.

However, instead of having to provide a list of values for the index, you can use a Python dictionary using the pd.Series() constructor. This way, the keys of the dictionary will become the index labels, and the values will be the data elements in the Series.

```
data = {'A':1, 'B':2, 'C':3, 'D':4, 'E':5}
series = pd.Series(data, name='Numbers')
print(series)
```

DataFrame

A DataFrame represents a structured, two-dimensional data table with columns that are labeled. It comprises a collection of individual entities, each carrying a specific value.

These values are organized in rows or records, and each column corresponds to a specific attribute.

To create a DataFrame, you use the pd.DataFrame() constructor, provided by the Pandas library. This constructor accepts diverse data types as input, but one of the most common ways of creating a DataFrame is by passing a dictionary as an argument.

```
data = {'name': ['Ann', 'Steve', 'Mary'], 'score':[77, 88, 93]}
df = pd.DataFrame(data)
print(df)
```

Output:

```
   name  score
0  Ann      77
1  Steve    88
2  Mary     93
```

Another way to generate DataFrames is by using lists. You can create a DataFrame by supplying one list for the rows and another list for the columns.

```
data = [['Ann', 77],['Steve', 88],['Mary', 93]]
df = pd.DataFrame(data, columns=['name', 'score'])
print(df)
```

Output:

```
   name  score
0  Ann      77
1  Steve    88
2  Mary     93
```

Reading data from files

In many cases, you won't need to generate the data manually. Instead, you will read data from files, particularly from CSV files.

To do this, you can use the built-in functions and methods designed for reading data from different file formats.

For example, if you want to read the CSV files, you can use the read_csv() function. By using this function, you can read the data from a CSV file and create a DataFrame easily.

```
df = pd.read_csv('employment.csv')
```

By default, read_csv() assumes that the CSV file has a header row containing column names. If your file does not have a header row, you can specify header=None and manually set the column names later.

```
df = pd.read_csv('employment.csv', header=None)
```

Once you have a DataFrame, you can explore and analyze the data using pandas' functions and methods.

You can use functions like head() or tail()to see the first few rows or last few rows respectively. By default, it shows the first 5 rows and the last 5 rows, but you can specify the number of rows to display.

```
df.head()
df.tail(3)
```

Also, you can use methods like describe() to obtain summary statistics of the numerical columns in the DataFrame, providing insights into the central tendency, dispersion, and distribution of the data.

```
df.describe()
```

Indexing and selecting

Most the things you will be doing with pandas is selecting specific values from a panda dataframe or series. Pandas provides various methods for indexing and selecting data based on specific criteria.

Selecting Columns

Let's say that you have a huge dataset containing lots of information, some of which might not be particularly relevant to your needs. Rather than tediously scrolling through this overwhelming amount of data, you can decide to select the particular aspects that truly matter to you.

This way, you can analyze those specific attributes more effectively and get the insights you need without getting lost in the sea of information.

You can use the dot notation to access a single column from the DataFrame as if it were an attribute of the DataFrame.

This method is particularly useful when the column name is a valid Python identifier. To select a column using dot notation, you simply write the DataFrame name followed by a dot and the column name.

```
result = df.Period
print(result)
```

However, you can use the square brackets to select one or more columns by passing a list of column names inside the brackets.

```
result = df[['Period', 'Magnitude']]
print(result)
```

This method is more flexible than the dot notation and allows you to select multiple columns simultaneously or when the column names are not valid Python identifiers.

Selecting Rows

Even though you can select specific columns from a dataset, it's often more practical to view just a few rows of the DataFrame to get a quick overview of the contents. By doing so, you can see how the data is structured, check for any potential issues, and determine the types of data present.

There are various ways of selecting rows in pandas including:

- Integer-based indexing using .iloc
- Label-based indexing using .loc
- Boolean indexing

Integer-based indexing using .iloc

Pandas provides a special attribute called iloc, which stands for integer location. With this attribute, you can access the rows and columns based on their integer positions or positional indices within the DataFrame.

This can be particularly useful when dealing with large datasets where you want to perform operations without worrying about the row labels.

In order to access rows or columns with iloc, you are required to provide the row and column positions as integers, lists or slices.

Here is the syntax:

dataframe.iloc[row_indices, column_indices]

The row_indices parameter represents the integer positions of the rows you want to select, and the column_indices parameter represents the integer positions of the columns you want to select.

You can provide single integers or slices for row_indices to access specific rows or a range of rows, respectively.

```
#selecting the row at index 0
result = df.iloc[0]
print(result)

#selecting the rows with slicing
result = df.iloc[0:3]
print(result)

#selecting selected rows
result = df.iloc[[1,2,5]]
print(result)
```

In the above example, only the row_indices are provided while the column_indices are omitted. By excluding the column_indices, you retrieve the specified rows for all columns.

Now, to retrieve specific columns from a DataFrame, you have to follow this syntax:

dataframe.iloc[:, columns]

The colon (:) before the comma signifies that we aim to select all rows in the DataFrame.

The following example demonstrates how to fetch the columns from a DataFrame:

```
#selecting a specific column
result = df.iloc[:, 0]
print(result)

#selecting a range of columns
result = df.iloc[:, 0:3]
print(result)

#selecting selected columns
result = df.iloc[:, [1,3,5]]
print(result)
```

However, if you want to select specific rows and columns together from a DataFrame using iloc, you can do so by combining both row indices and column indices separated by a comma.

```
#selecting rows and columns
result = df.iloc[0:10, 1:4]
print(result)
```

Label based selection using .loc

The .loc attribute provides a powerful and flexible way to access specific rows and columns based on their index labels. While iloc is based on integer positions, .loc uses row and column labels.

This is particularly useful if you are working with labeled data and need to access rows and columns using their meaningful labels.

When using the .loc attribute, you are required to provide the index labels of the rows you want to access. For accessing specific rows, you can pass a single index label, a list of index labels, or a slice of index labels.

```
#selecting the row at index label
result = df.loc['Name']
print(result)

#selecting selected rows
result = df.loc[['Name', 'Subject']]
print(result)
```

Also, you can specify the column labels to access specific columns in the entire DataFrame.

```
#selecting rows and columns
result = df.loc['Name', ['Subject', 'Period']]
print(result)
```

Boolean indexing

Boolean indexing allows you to select rows based on a condition or a set of conditions. You create a boolean mask, which is a series of True and False values, by applying a condition to one or more columns in the DataFrame. Then, you use this mask to filter the rows that meet the condition.

Take a look at this example:

```
#boolean indexing
result = df[df['Period'] > 2023]
print(result)

#the same thing as
result = df.loc[df['Period'] > 2023]
print(result)
```

In the above example, the result will produce a DataFrame containing only the rows where the value in the 'Period' column is greater than 2023.

The two methods are equivalent when used with boolean indexing, and they both result in the same filtered DataFrame based on the specified condition.

Assigning values in a DataFrame

Pandas allows you to modify the data within a DataFrame by assigning new values to its cells, columns, or rows. This is useful when you want to update, change, or add data to your DataFrame.

You can assign values to a single cell by specifying its row and column location. You can also assign values to an entire column, updating all its values at once. Furthermore, you can perform assignments selectively based on specific conditions using boolean indexing or other techniques.

The following examples demonstrate how to select and assign values to DataFrames in pandas.

```
# Assigning a value to entire 'Subject' column
df['Subject'] = "Languages"

# Assigning a row using iloc
df.iloc[2] = "Nothing to show"

# Assigning values based on conditions
df.loc[df['Scores'] > 69, 'Student'] = "A"

# Performing arithmetic assignment
df['Score'] = df['Score'] + 10
```

Sorting Data

Pandas provides the sort_values() function to sort a DataFrame based on one or more columns. You can specify the column(s) to sort by and the sort in ascending or descending order.

```
result = df.sort_values('Period')
print(result)
```

To sort a DataFrame in descending order based on a specific column, you can use the sort_values() function and set the ascending parameter to False.

```
result = df.sort_values('Period', ascending=False)
print(result)
```

Data Cleaning Functions

In real-world scenarios, data frequently exhibits missing values, duplicates, incorrect entries, and various other issues that may lead to erroneous conclusions. Dealing with these challenges requires performing data cleaning operations, which involve identifying and rectifying errors, inconsistencies, and inaccuracies in raw data to enhance its quality and reliability.

Pandas simplifies the data cleaning process by providing powerful tools that allow users to perform common data cleaning tasks efficiently.

For instance, to remove missing data, you can use functions as dropna() to remove rows with missing values or fillna() to replace missing values with specified values.

```
cleaned_df = df.dropna()
print(cleaned_df)

result = df.fillna('Nothing to show')
print(result)
```

Also, you can detect and remove duplicate rows using methods like drop_duplicates().

```
result = df.drop_duplicates()
print(result)
```

Data Aggregation

Data aggregation is an important technique in data analysis and statistics. It allows you to combine and summarize lots of data points or rows into just one representative value or maybe even a set of values. It's like condensing all that information into a neat and easy to use format.

The purpose of data aggregation is to make the data less complicated and find important information from it. By aggregating data, large datasets can be condensed into more manageable and informative summaries.

The first step in data aggregation is to create groups based on one or more columns of the DataFrame and then calculate summary statistics or apply custom functions to each group independently.

Take a look at this example:

```
data = {
    'Student': ['Andrew', 'Jane', 'Eve', 'Andrew', 'Jane', 'Eve'],
    'Subject': ['Maths', 'Maths', 'Maths', 'English', 'English',
      'English'],
    'Score': [85, 78, 92, 64, 91, 76]
}

df = pd.DataFrame(data)
```

To group your data based on a specific column, employ the .groupby() method and supply the desired column as an argument. Once the grouping is complete, you'll obtain a GroupBy object. To extract the 'Score' column from each group, simply access it using indexing with ['Score'].

```
result = df.groupby('Student')['Score']
```

If you run this code, you will get the following output:

	Student	Subject	Score
0	Andrew	Maths	85
1	Jane	Maths	78
2	Eve	Maths	92
3	Andrew	English	64
4	Jane	English	91
5	Eve	English	76

Now, at this stage, you can apply various aggregate functions to get insights into the grouped data, such as calculating. You apply an aggregation function such as sum(), mean(), count() and more to compute some summary statistics for each group.

```
print(result.sum())
print(result.mean())
print(result.count())
```

Output:
Student
Andrew   149
Eve   168
Jane   169
Name: Score, dtype: int64

Student
Andrew   74.5
Eve   84.0
Jane   84.5
Name: Score, dtype: float64

Student
Andrew   2
Eve   2
Jane   2
Name: Score, dtype: int64

Data Visualization with Matplotlib

Once you've completed the process of fetching and analyzing data, the natural next step is to visually present the information. By employing data visualization techniques, raw numbers and statistics can be transformed into captivating visual representations.

These visualizations not only enhance accessibility in data analysis but also bring forth valuable insights and patterns.

Data visualization serves as the key technique for converting raw data into compelling visual displays, which unveil inherent patterns, trends, and relationships within the dataset.

Python offers various libraries for data visualization, and among them, Matplotlib stands out as an exceptionally versatile and widely used tool. Matplotlib empowers users to generate popular visualization types, including line plots, scatter plots, histograms, and more.

Installing matplotlib

To use Matplotlib in your programs or projects, you first need to install it. You can do this by running the following command in your terminal or command prompt:

```
pip install matplotlib
```

Once you have successfully installed the library, you can easily import it into your program and start utilizing its functionalities right away.

```
import matplotlib
```

However, in most cases, you'll be using the pyplot interface of Matplotlib, which provides a simple and easy-to-use interface for creating various types of plots. To do this, you import Matplotlib's pyplot module using the alias "plt".

```
import matplotlib.pyplot as plt
```

> **Pro Tip:**
> *Matplotlib can work seamlessly with other Python libraries commonly used in data analysis, like NumPy and pandas. You can import these libraries into your script as needed and use their functionalities along with Matplotlib to manipulate data and create insightful visualizations.*

Visualizing with matplotlib

Before you can create visualizations, you have to get your data ready and at the same time, ensure that it is free from errors or missing values. By completing these preparatory processes, you set a solid foundation for meaningful and insightful data visualizations.

Once your data is ready, you can then proceed by importing the Matplotlib.

```
import matplotlib.pyplot as plt

months = [1,2,3,4,5,6,7,8,9,10,11,12]
avg_temp = [10, 12, 15, 20, 25, 28, 30, 28, 25, 20, 15, 12]
```

By importing this library, you will be able to create a wide variety of visualizations, from basic line charts to complex 3D plots.

Matplotlib works with a hierarchical structure of figures and axes. You start by creating a figure to serve as a window or page where your plot will be displayed. You can think of it as a big drawing board.

```
# Create a figure
fig = plt.figure()
```

Within the figure, you can add one or more axes, which represent the individual plotting areas where your charts will be drawn.

```
#Create axes within the figure
ax = fig.add_subplot(1, 1, 1)
```

By using the add_subplot() method of the figure object, you create an individual subplot (axes) within figure. This method requires that you provide the number of rows and columns in the subplot grid, along with the index or position of the subplot you want to create.

In this case, the arguments (1, 1, 1) indicate that you are creating a single subplot within a 1x1 grid. This means the figure will have only one row and one column, and the subplot will occupy the entire figure. The index 1 specifies that this subplot will be the first subplot in the grid.

Once you have your figure and axes set up, you can begin plotting your data using various plotting.

To generate a line plot, you can use the plot() function and the basic syntax is as follows:

plt.plot(x_data, y_data, format_string, **kwargs)

The x_data corresponds to the input data for the x-axis, while the y_data corresponds to the input data for the y-axis. The format_string argument, which is optional, allows you to define the style of the plot using a string that combines color, marker, and line style codes.

Also, **kwargs is used to provide extra keyword arguments for further customization of the plot, such as linewidth, markersize, label, and more.

Now, let's create a basic line plot.

In this case, the input data for x axis is the months for the year, while the input data for y axis is the average temperature for the month.

```
ax.plot(months, avg_temp)
```

At this point, you have successfully created a line plot and to see the plot, you can invoke the plt.show() function.

```
# Show the plot
plt.show()
```

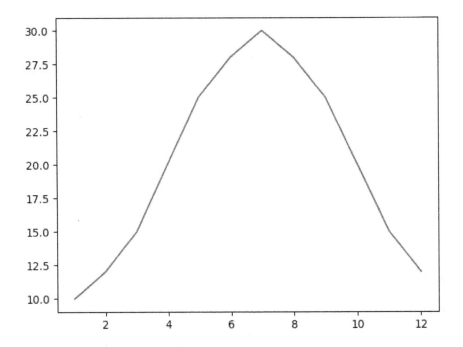

Creating other plots

Apart from the line plots, you can create a whole lot other types of plots. You can explore various functions such as scatter() for scatter plots, bar() for bar plots, hist() for histograms, and more to create different types of visualizations.

For instance, to create a bar plot, you can use the bar() method from the library, as illustrated in the example below:

```
#Bar chart
plt.bar(months, avg_temp)
plt.show()
```

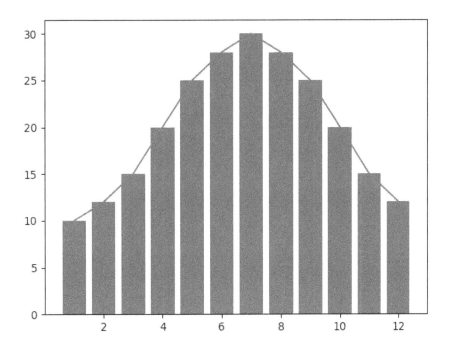

Customizing your plots

A lot of times, you may want to have your graphs and charts look more attractive and easier to understand. For example, by choosing suitable colors, labels, and font sizes, you can make the graph easier to read. You can adjust the way the graph looks by changing the range of the numbers on the sides, adding helpful marks, or writing extra explanations so people can understand it better.

To do all this, you have various options to customize the appearance of the graph, like choosing colors, line styles, marker shapes, giving the graph a title, adding labels to the axes, showing a grid, and more.

Now, let's customize the previous line plot to look to more professional and visually appealing.

```python
ax.plot(months, avg_temp, color='red', linewidth=2, marker='o',
markersize=8)
ax.set_xlabel('X-axis')
ax.set_ylabel('Y-axis')
ax.set_title('Average Monthly Temperature for 2021')

plt.show()
```

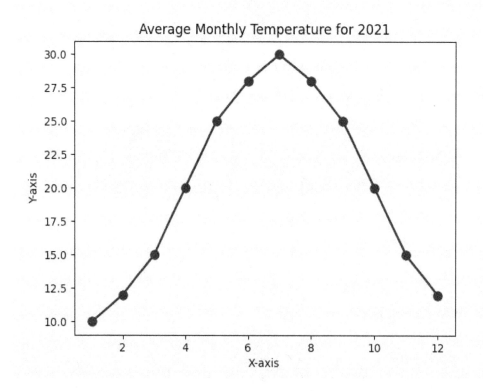

The above example illustrates the process of customizing a plot by defining its attributes, such as color, line width, markers, and marker size. It involves using the methods set_xlabel(), set_ylabel(), and set_title() to label the x-axis as "X-axis," the y-axis as "Y-axis," and give the plot the title "Average Monthly Temperature for 2021."

Summary

This chapter began by introducing the basics of data science and the various libraries in Python for data science. You learnt how to use the NumPy and Pandas libraries for data manipulation and analysis. Also, you learnt how to visualize data using Matplotlib.

Practice Exercises

1. Explain the growing popularity of data science in so many industries.
2. Mention popular python libraries for data science.
3. What is Numpy used for?
4. What are the advantages of Numpy arrays over Python lists?
5. Print a range between 1 and 100 using the Numpy.
6. Write a program that counts the number of times each value appears in a Numpy array of integers.
7. How do you identify and deal with missing values in Numpy?
8. How is pandas used in data science?
9. Differentiate between a Series and DataFrame in Pandas.
10. What are the different types of data sources in pandas?
11. State the different ways a DataFrame can be created in Pandas.
12. How to convert a Numpy array to a DataFrame of given shape?
13. Explain the difference between iloc and loc in pandas
14. What is the difference between Numpy and Pandas?
15. What is data aggregation?
16. Explain what you understand by data visualization and why is it important.
17. How do you create a line plot in matplotlib?
18. What are the various ways you can customize a plot in matplotlib?
19. How do you create a histogram using matplotlib?
20. How do you create a bar chart in matplotlib?

BUILDING WEB APPS WITH DJANGO

"Fiction is like a spider's web, attached ever so slightly perhaps, but still attached to life at all four corners. Often the attachment is scarcely perceptible."

- Virginia Woolf

A majority of the world's population relies on internet for education, business, entertainment, and social interactions. It has revolutionized the way we access information, connect with others, and conduct various activities. In fact, it has become an essential aspect of the modern society.

If you're a software developer and you can't write a program that can be accessed over the web, then you are missing out. The good news is that there are numerous frameworks and libraries available in Python that can help you build applications specifically designed to run on the internet.

One popular web application framework in Python is Django.

Learning outcome

In this chapter, you will learn:
- Web development basics.
- Django's fundamental concepts, such as models, views, and templates.
- To develop web applications using the Django framework.

Websites and web applications

Web applications are software programs or interactive websites that users can interact with. They can perform various tasks, such as sending and receiving data, processing user input, and displaying dynamic content.

These applications are typically accessed through web browsers like Google Chrome, Mozilla Firefox, or Safari.

While websites primarily consist of static web pages providing information, web applications differ significantly. A website is a collection of related web pages that provide content and information to visitors. Most of the times, they are static, displaying the same information to every visitor.

On the other hand, a web application is interactive and more complex. They are often dynamic, offering personalized and interactive experiences.

Examples of web applications include online banking systems, social media platforms, and online productivity tools and much more.

Both websites and web applications primarily function to serve web pages to users, utilizing the Hypertext Transfer Protocol (HTTP).

Hypertext Transfer Protocol, operates as a stateless protocol. This means that each client to server request is treated as an independent, isolated transaction without any knowledge of previous requests.

Pro Tip:
HTTP was designed this way intentionally for simplicity and scalability, making it easier for many users to interact with web servers without the server having to remember every detail about each user.

It doesn't know who you are based on your previous requests. It doesn't remember your preferences or past interactions. Each request you send is like introducing yourself all over again.

Users begin by accessing the web application through a web browser (such as Chrome, Firefox, Safari) or a mobile app. They can do this by entering the application's URL in the address bar or by clicking on a link from a search engine, social media, or another website.

When the user enters the URL and presses Enter, the web browser sends a request to the web server where the application is hosted. This request is typically made using the HTTP or HTTPS protocol.

The web server receives the request and processes it. This might involve querying a database, running specific code, or retrieving files. The server generates an appropriate response based on the user's request.

The server sends the generated response back to the user's web browser. This response contains HTML, CSS, JavaScript, and other assets necessary to render the web page.

Then, the web browser receives the response and interprets the HTML, CSS, and JavaScript to render the web page. This includes displaying text, images, forms, buttons, and other elements that make up the user interface of the web application.

Users interact with the web application through the rendered user interface. They can click on buttons, fill out forms, submit data, or perform various other actions depending on the functionality provided by the application.

Web development with Python

Python is known for its versatility, and one of the popular uses is in creating web applications. It has a variety of web frameworks that simplify the process of building web applications.

A web framework is a collection of structured sets of tools and libraries that assist developers in building web applications more efficiently. They simplify the process by offering pre-defined structures, functionalities, and tools, allowing developers to focus more on the specific features of their applications rather than reinventing the underlying mechanisms required for web development.

Python offers numerous web development frameworks, such as Django, Flask, Tornado, and Pyramid. Each framework has its unique features and is suited for different types of web applications. These frameworks offer built-in features such as URL routing, form management, and database communication.

However, Django happens to be a popular choice by many developers for building any kind of web application and in this chapter, you will be learning how to build web applications using Django. In this chapter, you will build a simple job posting board web application using Django.

Understanding the Django Framework

Django is a popular Python framework for web development and is known for its simplicity, flexibility, and scalability, making it an excellent choice for building web applications of all sizes.

It follows the *"Don't Repeat Yourself"* (DRY) principles, which is a software development concept that promotes the idea of reducing redundancy in code. Instead of writing the same code multiple times in different parts of a program, you write it once and refer back to it whenever you need that particular piece of code.

This principle promotes the idea of avoiding repetition and redundancy in software development. This leads to more maintainable, less error-prone, and efficient code because changes can be made in one place without having to update multiple copies of the same code.

Django comes with a wide range of built-in features and libraries, such as an ORM (Object-Relational Mapping), authentication, templating engine, admin interface, and more.

It has been used to develop a wide range of popular web applications and websites across various domains.

The following are some of the popular apps developed with Django:

- Instagram
- Pinterest
- Dropbox
- Eventbrite
- Disqus

Installing Django

Before building web applications with Django, it's important that you set up your development environment. This means organizing your tools and software in a way that allows you to easily locate the necessary files and tools while working on the project. This not only ensures an organized development environment but also ensures the stability, security, and manageability of your projects.

This involves several steps but let's start by setting up a virtual environment.

Setting Up a Virtual Environment

A virtual environment is an isolated environment in your computer where you can install libraries and packages specific to a particular project, without affecting the system -wide Python installation. In other words, it's a special area on your computer where you can set up all the packages or libraries that a specific project needs.

For example, one project might require a specific version of the library, while another project might need a higher version. If you install both versions directly into your computer's main system, they might conflict and cause problems. But with a virtual environment, you create a separate space for each project.

> **Pro Tip:**
> *It's a good practice to create a virtual environment specifically for that project. This way, you ensure that the libraries and dependencies you use for a specific project is isolated from other projects or Python Installations.*

To create a virtual environment, you can follow these steps in your terminal or command prompt.

I. Create a project directory or folder for your project

This step involves creating a designated folder or directory on your computer where all the files related to your Django project will be stored. You can do this by using the following commands in your terminal or command prompt.

```
mkdir my_django_project
```

This command creates a directory or folder named "my_django_project" in the current location.

This will become the main container for your Django project files.

> **Pro Tip:**
> *The mkdir command stands for "make directory" and is used to create a new folder with the specified name.*

2. Use the cd command to move to your project folder

Having created a project directory, the next thing to do is to use the cd command to navigate to the project folder as shown below:

```
cd my_django_project
```

3. Create a virtual environment

Now that you are inside the project directory, you can then create a virtual environment.

To create a virtual environment, use the following command:

```
python -m venv venv
```

When you execute this command in your terminal or command prompt within your project directory, it will create a dedicated virtual environment folder within your project folder, named according to what you specified (venv or any other chosen name).

This virtual environment will contain a separate Python interpreter and copies of essential libraries needed for your project.

4. Activate the virtual environment

After making a virtual environment, the next step is to activate it. The process of activating a virtual environment is different depending on the operating system you're using (such as Windows, macOS, or Linux). Each operating system has its own command or script for activating the virtual environment.

For example:

On Windows:
```
venv\Scripts\activate
```

On macOS and Linux:
```
source venv/bin/activate
```

Once the virtual environment is activated, any Python-related command you run in the terminal or command prompt will use the Python version and packages from the virtual environment

When the virtual environment is activated, you'll see the virtual environment's name in your terminal or command prompt, indicating that you are now working within the virtual environment.

5. Install Django

Now that your virtual environment is active, you can install Django using pip by running the following command in your terminal or command prompt:

```
pip install django
```

This command downloads and installs the latest version of Django into your virtual environment.

Creating a Django Project

With Django installed, it's time to create your project. A project is a collection of settings, configurations, and files for a specific web application.

But first, it's essential to make sure that you're in the right directory or navigate to the desired directory where you want to create your Django project.

Once you're in the correct directory, you can run the following command:

```
django-admin startproject myproject
```

When you execute this command in your terminal or command prompt, Django will generate the basic structure for your project inside a new directory named "myproject".

Inside your project directory, you'll find the file manage.py and another directory with the same name as your project.

This inner directory contains the actual project files, including settings, URL configurations, and the project's main Python package.

You can navigate into the newly created project directory using the cd command and run the development server:

```
cd myproject
python manage.py runserver
```

After you run python manage.py runserver, the terminal will display a message that includes a URL, usually http://localhost:8000/.

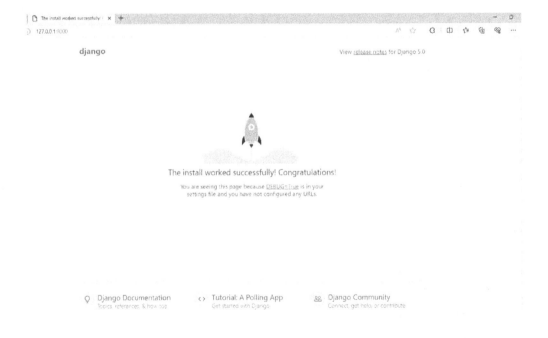

Alternatively, you can open your web browser and type in the address http://localhost:8000/ in the address bar.

> **Pro Tip:**
> *The "localhost" refers to your own computer, while port 8000 is the default port on which the Django development server runs.*

Django Project Structure

Django organizes projects in a structured manner, guaranteeing that they are well-arranged, easily manageable, and capable of expanding smoothly as the application grows.

Although Django provides a standard project structure, you have the flexibility to customize it according to your project's specific needs and demands.

Here's an overview of the standard Django project structure:

```
projectname/
        manage.py
        projectname/
                init.py
                settings.py
                urls.py
                wsgi.py
```

projectname/

This directory holds the entire Django project. It's named after the project and contains another directory with the same name. The inner directory serves as a Python package, organizing the various components and project configuration files related to the project.

manage.py

This is a command-line utility that allows you to interact with various aspects of your Django project, such as running development servers, creating database migrations, and managing the application.

Project Configuration Files

settings.py: This file contains all the project settings and configuration options, such as database settings, installed apps, middleware, and more. It's a central place to configure your Django project.

wsgi.py: This is a Python file within a Django project that serves as an entry point for running the Django application on a Web Server Gateway Interface (WSGI) compatible web server.

> **Pro Tip:**
> *WSGI is a specification for how a web server communicates with web applications written in Python.*

urls.py: This file defines the URL patterns for your project. It maps URLs to views and allows Django to route incoming requests to the appropriate view functions.

Apps

In Django, applications or "apps" help organize and separate your project's functionalities into smaller, reusable parts called "apps." Each app usually operates independently and focuses on a specific feature or aspect of the overall project. These apps have separate directory structures for organizing specific files and functionalities, including:

models.py: This file essentially serves as a blueprint for the database tables and relationships used by the app. With the "models.py" file, you can define the various data components, such as fields, relationships between different types of data, constraints, and other characteristics required for their application's database.

Django then uses this information to automatically create the corresponding database tables and manage interactions with the database based on the defined models.

views.py: Views are responsible for handling HTTP requests and returning HTTP responses. This file contains the view functions or classes that define the application's behaviour.

urls.py: This file defines the URL patterns specific to the app .

Creating the Django Job Board Project

The previous project we developed served as a basic example to illustrate the process of building a project in Django. Now, we're moving on to create a more realistic web application. With this app, you can be able to post, view, update or delete job vacancies.

However, before proceeding, it's advisable to set up a project folder and create a virtual environment using the steps outlined below.

Step 1: Set Up a Project Folder

Create a new directory or folder for your Django project. You can name it whatever you like. Using the cd command, you can navigate into the directory from your terminal or command prompt.

```
mkdir job_board_project
cd job_board_project
```

Step 2: Create a Virtual Environment

You can create and activate a virtual environment as shown below:

```
python -m venv venv
```

Activate virtual environment on Windows:
```
venv\Scripts\activate
```

Activate virtual environment on macOS and Linux:
```
source venv/bin/activate
```

Step 3: Install Django

Now that your virtual environment is active, you can install Django using pip by running the following command in your terminal or command prompt:

```
pip install django
```

Step 4: Create a Django Project

Once Django is installed, you can create a new Django project using the following command:

```
django-admin startproject job_board_project
```

When you run this command, Django creates a new directory called "job_board_project" in your current location.

Step 5: Verify Your Django Project

Once you've completed the previous steps, you'll notice a collection of Django files and folders within your project directory. To ensure that your project is configured accurately, proceed to run the development server by executing the command:

```
python manage.py runserver
```

This will start the development server. You can access your Django project by opening a web browser and visiting http://127.0.0.1:8000/.

Creating the Job Board App

After creating the job_board_project, the next step is to create a job board app using the following steps.

First, navigate to the root directory of your Django project using the cd command in your terminal or command prompt.

```
cd job_board_project
```

You can create a new app using the startapp management command followed by the name of your app. For example, if you want to create an app called job_board, run the following command:

```
python manage.py startapp job_board
```

Once the app is created, you'll find a new directory with the name of your app in your project directory. Inside this directory, you'll see several files and folders that Django has generated for you.

Integrate your app with your project

To make Django aware of your new app, add its name to the INSTALLED_APPS list in your project's settings.py file. Open settings.py in your project folder and locate the INSTALLED_APPS section. Add your app's name like this:

```
INSTALLED_APPS = [
'job_board',
...
```

]

This tells Django that your project will be using the functionality provided by the "job_board" app.

Having created the job board app and included it in the settings file, you can now create models, views, and templates.

Defining the Job Model

When you're building a web application with Django, you often need a way to store and manage data. That's where models come in. Models in Django are Python classes that define the structure and behaviour of your data.

They serve as blueprints for organizing and managing data within an application, guiding both its structure and functionality while facilitating interaction with the database. Each model class outlines specific fields that correspond to table columns and incorporates methods for database operations.

Before coding the actual models, you need to identify the kind of data you need. This process involves creating entities that mirror the desired data types, defining their attributes, with each attribute representing a column in the database.

> **Pro Tip:**
> *An entity is like a virtual object or concept that represents something in the real world.*

When you create a model, Django automatically generates the database schema based on your model definitions. It knows how to translate your Python code into database tables, creating the necessary tables, defining columns, and establishing relationships between tables, all according to your model specifications.

This automation saves you a lot of manual database setup work, allowing you to focus more on developing your application's features and less on database management intricacies.

Now, let's define a Job model which represents the individual job postings or vacancies.

> **Pro Tip:**
> *These attributes define the structure of the Job model, specifying the types of data*

that can be stored for each company record in the database. Django applications often contain a models.py file where you define database models for that specific app.

Now, open the models.py file within the job_board app. By default, the following line of code should be in your model.py file.

```
from django.db import models
# Define fields here
```

Next, define a Python class named Job that inherits from models.Model.

```
class Job(models.Model):
```

Within your model class, you can define various class variables to represent the fields of your database table. These fields could be things like a person's name, age, email and so on.

Pro Tip:
Django provides a variety of field classes like CharField (for character fields), IntegerField (for whole numbers), DateField (for date values), ForeignKey (for creating relationships with other models), and so on. You choose the appropriate field class based on the type of data you want to store in that particular field. For each field, you can specify various options according to your requirements. These options include things like max_length (for CharField to specify the maximum length of the string), null (to specify if the field can be NULL in the database), blank (to specify if a field is allowed to be empty in forms), and many others. For example, if you want to store an optional email address, you might use CharField with null=True and blank=True options.

Now, let's define the Job model in the job_board app.

```
from django.db import models

class Job(models.Model):
    title = models.CharField(max_length=100)
    description = models.TextField()
    company = models.CharField(max_length=100)
```

```
created_at = models.DateTimeField(auto_now_add=True)
```

The Job model represents the individual job postings or vacancies. It defines the structure of a job listing. It specifies what attributes each job listing will have, such as title, description, company and created date.

- **title:** A character field representing the title of the job listing.
- **description:** A text field representing the detailed description of the job.
- **company:** A character field representing companies where vacancies exist.
- **created_at:** A date-time field representing the date and time when the job listing was published.

Models' methods

In object-oriented programming, fields serve as attributes of the class, while methods serve as behaviours. By including methods, you can define how the models behave.

A common method to include in a model is the str() method, allowing you to define how objects are represented as strings.

```
class Job(models.Model):
    title = models.CharField(max_length=100)
    description = models.TextField()
    company = models.CharField(max_length=100)
    created_at = models.DateTimeField(auto_now_add=True)

    def __str__(self):
        return self.title
```

Run Migrations

A migration is a script that defines the changes to be made in the database schema. It includes operations like creating tables, modifying existing tables, or deleting tables.

When you run migrations for the first time in Django, you typically initialize the database schema based on the models you've defined in your Django application. This involves creating database tables and relationships as specified in your Django models.

So, navigate to your Django project directory in the terminal or command prompt and execute the following command.

```
python manage.py makemigrations
```

When you run the above command, Django inspects the models in your project and detects any changes that have been made since the last migration. It then generates migration files that represent these changes.

After creating the migration files, you need to apply these changes to the database.

```
python manage.py migrate
```

The above command will create it or generate tables based on your application's models. Each model corresponds to a table in the database, and the model's fields become columns in the table.

If the database already exists and you've modified your models (like adding, changing, or removing fields), running migrations will update the existing database structure to match these changes. If you don't have a database, Django will automatically create an SQLite database for you. If you already have one, Django will modify it accordingly.

> **Pro Tip:**
> *Django supports various database types, like PostgreSQL, MySQL, SQLite, and Oracle. You can configure the database type in the project's settings.py file using the DATABASES setting.*

Adding records and querying the Database

Django comes with a powerful feature known as the Object-Relational Mapping (ORM) that allows programmers to interact with databases using Python code instead of raw SQL queries.

This ORM tool enables developers to interact with databases using Python code. With ORM, you can execute a wide range of queries on the database, such as filtering data based on specific criteria, sorting records, and performing aggregations.

Every database table is represented by a Python class called a model. Each model has a manager often referred to as objects and these objects provides a set of methods for querying the database.

In other words, managers allow you to perform complex database operations without having to write raw SQL queries.

So, in your terminal type the following to start the interactive session.

```
python manage.py shell
```

This command starts an interactive Python shell session. By having this interactive environment, you can test database queries, manipulate data, and perform various tasks related to your Django project.

Now that the interactive session is running, you can import the Job model as shown below:

```
from job_board.models import Job
```

Then, you can proceed by using the create() method to create a new record and save the record in the database.

```
Job.objects.create(
                title='Software Developer', company='XYZ',
                description='Description of an example company'
                )
```

Output:
<Job: Software Developer>

This method creates a new instance of the Job model, populates it with the provided values, and saves it to the database.

Also, you can create a new instance of the model, populate its fields, and then save it to the database using the save() method.

```
# Create a new job instance
job = Job(
     title='Software Developer', company='XYZ',
     description='Description of an example company'
     )

# Save the new job to the database
```

```
job.save()
```

Both methods achieve the same result. The choice between them depends on your preference and the specific context of your application.

To query the database, you can use the all() and filter() methods of the object to retrieve data from the Job table as shown below:.

```
# Retrieve all jobs
jobs = Job.objects.all()
jobs
companies
```

Output
<QuerySet [<Job: Software Developer>, <Job: Software Developer>]>

The object.all() method retrieves all records from the table corresponding to the model Job in the database.

You can filter jobs based on specific criteria using the filter() method.

```
# Filter jobs based on title
jobs = Job.objects.filter( title='Software Developer')
jobs
```

<QuerySet [<Job: Software Developer>, <Job: Software Developer>]>

To retrieve a single job by a specific attribute, for instance, title, you can use the get() method. However, keep in mind that the get() should be used when you expect exactly one result.

```
job = Job.objects.get(title='Software Developer')
job
```

<Job: Software Developer>

Creating Views

Views in Python represent functions or classes designed to accept a web request and produce a web response. These views serve as containers for the application's core logic, responsible for managing and processing incoming HTTP requests.

They dictate the content to present to users and manage the handling of form submissions, executing various tasks such as:

- Querying the database to retrieve data.
- Processing user input from forms.
- Performing calculations or data transformations.

Views can be linked to distinct HTTP methods like GET, POST, PUT, DELETE, among others. For instance, one view may be designated to exhibit a list of items by utilizing a GET request, while another view handles form submissions through a POST request.

There exist two primary classifications of views: Function-Based Views (FBV) and Class-Based Views (CBV). Nonetheless, the emphasis of this book solely centers on class-based views.

Class-Based Views (CBV)

Traditionally, views have been written as functions. However, with the growing complexity of web applications, developers needed improved methods to structure their code more efficiently.

Class-Based Views offer an interesting alternative, allowing for the creation of classes that encapsulate common functionalities.

To create a class-based view, you need to define a Python class that inherits from Django's View class.

Take a look at this example:

```
from django.http import HttpResponse
from django.views import View

class MyView(View):
    def get(self, request):
```

Django provides a wide range of built-in class-based views for common use cases, such as displaying forms, handling CRUD (Create, Read, Update, Delete) operations, and rendering templates.

TemplateView: Renders a template and delivers an HTTP response.
ListView: Generates a display of objects retrieved from a database query as a list.
DetailView: Renders detailed information about a specific object retrieved from a database query.
CreateView: Manages the creation of new objects within the system.
UpdateView: Controls the modification of existing objects in the system.
DeleteView: Handles the removal of objects from the system.

Creating views for the job_board project

This involves defining classes that handle HTTP requests and return appropriate responses.

So, within the views.py file of the job_board app, define the following view:

```
from django.views.generic import ListView
from .models import Job

class JobListView(ListView):
    model = Job
    template_name = 'job_board/index.html'
    context_object_name = 'job_list'
```

The above defines a class-based view called JobListView, which operates on the Job model. It specifies the template file ('job_board/index.html') and the context variable name ('job_list') to be used for rendering the view.

URL Configurations

URL configurations are like a roadmap for websites. They tell the website's code which page or function to show when a specific web address (URL) is typed in or clicked on.

Also, they serve as a routing mechanism, directing incoming requests to the appropriate code handlers.

So, open the url.py file in the job_board project and replace the default content there with the following:

```python
from django.contrib import admin
from django.urls import path, include

urlpatterns = [
    path('admin/', admin.site.urls),
    path('', include('job_board.urls')),
]
```

The urlpatterns list contains two elements. The first element maps the URL pattern admin/ to the Django admin interface using admin.site.urls. This means that when users visit /admin/ in the browser, they will access the admin interface.

The second element maps the root URL of the project (/) to the URL patterns defined in the job_board.urls module using the include function.

Inside your app directory, create a urls.py file with the name urls.py. In this file, you define the URL patterns as shown below:

```python
from django.urls import path
from .views import JobListView


urlpatterns = [
    # Job URLs
    path('', JobListView.as_view(), name='job_list'),
]
```

Templates

After setting up the URL configurations, the next thing to do is to develop HTML templates associated with each view to render the user interface.

Pro Tip:

Django's template system allows you to create dynamic web pages by combining HTML with template tags, which interact with your views to display data. Templates allow you to separate the presentation layer from your application's logic, making your code more maintainable and promoting code reusability.

In your app directory, create a directory named "templates". Inside this directory, create a subfolder named after your app ("job_board"), and place your HTML files into this subfolder.

In this case, create a HTML file with the name index.hmtl to serve as the home page and the page for listing out the available job vacancies.

```html
<!DOCTYPE html>
<html lang="en">
<head>
  <meta charset="UTF-8">
  <meta name="viewport" content="width=device-width, initial-scale=1.0">
  <title>Job Board</title>
</head>
<body>
  <header>
    <h1>Latest Job Listings</h1>
    <nav>
      <ul>
        <li><a href="/">Home</a></li>
        <li><a href="/jobs">Browse Jobs</a></li>
      </ul>
    </nav>
  </header>

  <main>

      <h2>Job Listings</h2>
      <p>Job Title 1</p>
      <p>Job Title 2</p>
      <p>Job Title 3</p>

  </main>
```

```
</body>
</html>
```

Templating engine

Django's template language enables the dynamic generation of HTML content using data from your Django application. To integrate this language into your HTML file, you can use Django template tags enclosed in {% %} or {{ }}.

These tags facilitate the insertion of dynamic content or the control of template flow. For instance, you can iterate through a list of jobs using the {% for %} loop and display each job's title within <p> tags by accessing the title attribute of each job object from the job_list queryset.

Now, you can modify HTML to use Django's template language as shown below:

```
{% for job in job_list %}
    <p>{{job.title}}</p>
{% endfor %}
```

Admin Interface

Django's admin interface is a convenient way to manage your Django project's data models without having to write custom views and forms. It provides a built-in administrative interface for managing Django applications' data.

With minimal configuration, Django automatically generates a powerful administrative interface based on your application's models, enabling users to perform CRUD (Create, Read, Update, Delete) operations effortlessly.

To make your models editable in the admin interface, you need to register them with the admin site.

This is usually done in the admin.py file of your app.

```
from django.contrib import admin
from .models import Job
```

```
admin.site.register(Job)
```

However, you need a superuser account to access the admin interface.

Superuser account

A superuser is a special type of user in Django who has unrestricted access to all parts of the application, including the admin interface.

They have the ability to perform CRUD (Create, Read, Update, Delete) operations on any data within the application and can also manage other users and their permissions.

To create a superuser account in Django, you can use the createsuperuser management command.

Open your terminal, navigate to your Django project directory, and run the following code:

```
python manage.py createsuperuser
```

Follow the prompts to input a username, an email address, and a password for the superuser.

Once completed, the superuser account will be created, granting you full administrative privileges.

```
Username (leave blank to use 'user'): bonaakubue
Email address: bona@nanoedgeng.com
Password:
Password (again):
Superuser created successfully.
```

You can then log in to the Django admin interface using the created superuser credentials, providing access to manage all aspects of the Django project. To do this, start your Django development server and navigate to http://localhost:8000/admin in your web browser.

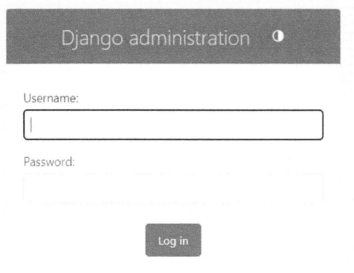

Once logged in, you'll see a list of registered models (in this case Jobs).

Click on the Jobs to view its entries. You can then click on the "Add" button to add a new entry.

You'll be presented with a form where you can input the details of the new entry. Fill in the necessary fields and click "Save" to add the entry. After saving, you should see the new entry listed among the existing entries for that model.

Add job

Title:

Description:

Company:

SAVE   Save and add another   Save and continue editing

Additionally, Django's admin interface also allows you to perform other CRUD operations including updating and deleting entries.

Now, if you refresh the home page of the app, the new entry will be indicated.

Latest Job Listings

- Home
- Browse Jobs

Job Listings

Software Developer

Software Developer

Content Writer

Static Contents

Static content refers to files that remain unchanged during the runtime of a web application. This includes images, CSS stylesheets, JavaScript files, fonts, and any other resources that do not depend on server-side processing.

Django provides flexible options for incorporating external libraries into your project. For instance, you can easily integrate Bootstrap into your Django project and leverage its powerful CSS and JavaScript components to create responsive and visually appealing web applications.

Deploying a Django

Deploying Django applications involves several steps, and the exact process may vary depending on your hosting platform and specific requirements. There are multiple hosting options, such as traditional web servers, Platform-as-a-Service (PaaS) providers like Heroku, and Infrastructure-as-a-Service (IaaS) providers like AWS and DigitalOcean.

Summary

This chapter began by introducing the basics of web development basics. It also introduced the fundamental concepts of the Django framework, which is a powerful web development framework for building dynamic and interactive web applications using Python. You learnt the basics of web development using Django's core concepts like models, views, and templates, develop web applications using Django.

Practice Exercises

1. Can you name some companies that use Django?
2. How do you create virtual environment in python and why is it important?
3. Explain the Django project directory structure.
4. What is the context in Django?
5. What's the significance of the settings.py file?
6. What are Django models and how are they used?
7. How to filter items in the Model?
8. Explain how you can set up the Database in Django.
9. What databases are supported by Django?
10. How do you use Django ORM to perform crud operations?

CONCLUSION

Congratulations! You have reached the end of this book. By completing this journey, you have taken your first steps into the exciting world of programming and gained a solid foundation in Python.

Throughout this book, we covered the fundamental concepts of programming, such as variables, data types, control structures, functions, and modules.

You have learnt how to manipulate and transform data, how to make decisions using conditional statements, and how to repeat actions using loops. We also explored more advanced topics like file handling, error handling, and object-oriented programming. Also, you have learnt how to use Python for data science and creating a web application.

This is the time to put your knowledge to work! This is the time to gain experience by using your knowledge to solve real world problems.

Knowledge is not enough. There is a great difference between knowing something and having experience in something.

That is the reason why you hear companies saying that they need people with 5years experience. 10 years' experience!

So, don't be in a hurry looking for a paid job. Instead strive to gain some experience.

Perhaps, you should consider contributing to an open-source project or work for someone for free. The experience that you will get doing the real work is so priceless.

The possibilities with Python are endless. Whether you want to build web applications, analyze data, automate tasks, or delve into artificial intelligence and machine learning, Python will be your trusted companion.

Good luck!

INDEX

A

Absolute Import, 140

Access Modes, 143

Accessing Arrays, 272

Adding And Removing, 274

Addition, 22, 26

Algebraic Expressions, 26

Anonymous, 129

Append() Method, 76

Apps, 310

Arange() Function, 268

Arguments, 127

Arithmetic Operators, 22, 24, 178

Asyncio Module, 199

Attributions, 228

B

Backspace Character, 64

Basic Data Types, 6

Beautiful Soup Library, 218

Binary, 7

Binary Data, 146

Binary Level, 31

Binary Numbers, 8

Bitiwse Not, 31

Bitwise And, 31

Bitwise AND Operator, 31

Bitwise Left Shift Operator, 35

Bitwise Leftshift, 31

Bitwise Operators, 31

Bitwise OR Operator, 32

Bitwise Right Shift, 31

Bitwise Right Shift Operator, 36

Bitwise Xor, 31

Bitwise XOR Operator, 33

Boolean Indexing, 273, 291

Boolean Values, 29

Booleans, 6, 7, 17

Break, 50

Break Statement, 50

Broadcasting, 280

Bytearrays, 148

C

Calculations, 23

Calling A Function, 122

Carriage Return Character, 64

Cartesian Product, 118

Cartesian Product Of Sets, 118

Categorize, 6

Characteristics, 19

Characters, 58

Children, 225

Class Variables, 160

Class-Based Views (CBV), 320

Clear() Method, 104

Closing A File, 146

Code, 33, 52

Code Organization, 135

Collaboration, 135

Combination Of Letters, 16

Complex Numbers, 6, 9

Composite Object, 173

Composition, 173

Compound Expressions, 20

Comprehension In Dictionaries, 109

Computer, 6, 173

Computer Program, 40

Concatenation, 54, 80

Conditional Statements, 41

Constructors, 159

Continue Statement, 51

Control Flow Statements, 41

Converting String To Bytearray, 149

Copy Files, 152

Copy() Method, 104

Coroutines, 200

Count() Function, 94

Createview, 321

Creating A Function, 122

Creating A Function With Parameters, 123

Creating A Session, 214

Creating A String, 54

Creating Data, 283

Creating Generators, 130

Creating Random Arrays, 279

Cryptographic Applications, 15

D

Daemon Threads, 242

Data, 6, 19

Data Aggregation, 293

Data Manipulation, 282

Data Science, 263, 264

Data Types, 6, 14

Data Validation, 227

Data Visualization, 295

Dataframe, 285, 291

Decimal Numbers, 8

Decode Function, 148

Decorator, 251

Del Keyword, 101

Del Statement, 101

Delete File, 153

Deleter Method, 252

Deleteview, 321

Deleting Attributes, 261

Deploying A Django, 326

Descriptor Methods, 258

Descriptors, 257

Desired Data, 220

Detailview, 321

Dictionaries, 6, 17, 98

Dictionary, 99, 109

Dictreader() Method, 151

Dictwriter(), 151

Difference, 115

Dimension, 270

Dimensional Array, 265

Dir() Function, 137

Directory, 139

Division, 22, 26

Django, 301, 302

Django Framework, 304

Django Project Structure, 308

Double Asterisk, 22

Double Forward Slash, 22

Dummy Variables, 92

Dynamic Attribute Retrieval, 259

E

Elif Statements, 43

Else Block, 188

Else Statement, 42

Encapsulation, 163

Enumerate() Method, 108

Equality, 27

Equality Operator, 28

Escape Characters, 64

Event Handlers, 200

Event Loops, 200

Except Block, 186

Exceptions, 185

Exponent, 70

Exponentiation, 22, 26

Expressions, 18, 29

F

False, 28

Falsey, 28

Fetch The Web Page, 219

File, 17, 142, 143

Filter() Function, 88

Finally Block, 188

Find() Method, 221

Find_All() Method, 222

Floating-Point, 22

Floats, 6, 9

Floor Division, 22

For Loop, 46

Format Function, 66

Format() Method, 14

Formfeed Character, 64

Formula, 34

Fractional Value, 12

Fromkeys() Method, 104

Frozen Sets, 119

F-Strings, 66, 67

G

Games, 15

Generator Expressions, 132

Generator Functions, 130

Get() Method, 105, 223

Getter And Setter Methods, 247

Getter Method, 252

Global Interpreter Lock, 244

Greater Or Equal To, 27

Greater Than, 27

H

Hexadecimal, 7

Hexadecimal Numbers, 8

HTTP, 303

HTTPS Protocol, 303

I

Identity Operators, 38

If Statements, 42

Imaginary Part, 9

Immutability Of Tuples, 93

Import Product, 119

Importing A Module, 135

Importing All Definitions, 135, 136

Importing Specific Names, 135

Importing With An Alias, 135

Index() Function, 95

Indexing, 54, 74, 272

Indexing And Selecting, 287

Information, 16

Inheritance, 170

Inheritance, 166

Input, 19

Input() Function, 19

Insert() Method, 77

Install Django, 305, 307

Installing Django, 305

Installing Matplotlib, 295

Installing Numpy, 266

Installing Pandas, 283

Instance Variables, 159

Instantiating A Class, 158

Integer Part, 13

Integer Value, 12

Integers, 6

Intersection, 115

Items() Method, 105

Itertools, 119

J

Job Board App, 312

Job Model, 313

JSON Contents, 212

Jump Statements, 41, 50

K

Keyboard, 173

Keys() Method, 106

Keyword Arguments, 124

L

Lambda Functions, 85

Lambda Functions, 129

Left Operand, 24

Legality, 227

Len() Function, 94

Less Or Equal, 27

Less Than, 27

List, 73

List Comprehension, 81, 85

Lists, 16, 17, 73

Listview, 321

Locks, 240

Log Levels, 230

Logging, 230

Logging Functions, 231

Logging In Python, 229

Logging To A File, 233

Logical Operators, 29

Logical Values, 17

Loop Prematurely, 52

Looping, 55

Looping A Dictionary, 102

Looping Statements, 41, 46

Looping Through Keys, 102

Looping Through Value, 103

M

Manage.Py, 309

Mangled Names, 165

Map, 85

Map() Function, 83

Map(), Zip() And Filter() Functions, 83

Mathematical Concepts, 9

Mathematical Expression, 25

Mathematical Functions, 11

Mathematical Operations, 277

Matplotlib, 295

Membership Operators, 37

Membership Test, 61

Methods, 161

Min() And Max(), 94

Minus Operator, 21

Models Methods, 315

Models.Py, 310

Module, 134

Module Search Path, 138

Modules, 135

Modulus, 22, 26

Move Files, 153

Multidimensional Array, 266

Multiple Exceptions, 187

Multiple Inheritance, 170

Multiplication, 22, 26

Multiplication Operator, 22, 24

N

Name Mangling, 165

Named Tuples, 96

Navigating The Trees, 224

Nested Comprehension, 83

Nested If Statements, 44

Not Equality, 27

Not Operator, 30

Np.Append() Function, 274

Np.Insert() Function, 275

Number Type Conversion, 10

Numbers, 6, 73

Numeric, 6, 7

Numeric Data, 6

Numpy, 264

O

Object-Oriented Programming, 156

Octal Numbers, 8

Old String Substitution, 66, 68

OOP, 157

Open () Function, 142

Operand, 24, 28

Operations On Sets, 114

Operations On Strings, 54

Operations On Tuples, 93

Operator Precedence, 20, 26

Operator Types, 20

Organization, 135

Organize, 6

Outcome, 117

Output, 18

Output:, 42, 76

Overriding A Class, 169

P

Package Import, 138

Packages, 138

Packing, 90

Pandas, 282, 283

Parameters, 126

Parent, 224

Parent Class, 169

Parentheses, 25, 26, 90

Parse The HTML, 220

Pass, 52

PEDMMAS, 26

Percentage Sign, 22

Planning, 184

Plots, 299

Pop(), 77

Pop() Method, 78, 101, 106

Popitem() Method, 101, 102, 107

Positional And Keyword Arguments, 124

Positional Arguments, 124

POST Request, 211

Precision, 70

Print() Function, 17

Process The Data, 221

Program Execution, 18

Programmers, 6

Project Configuration Files, 309

Projectname/, 309

PROPERTIES AND DESCRIPTORS, 245

Property, 251

Property Decorator, 252

Python, 6, 19, 21, 38, 41, 59, 68, 90, 134, 230, 244

Python Expression, 25

Python Library, 264

Python Programming, 10

Q

Query Parameter, 211

Query Strings, 211

Quotation Mark, 16, 67

Quotient, 23

R

Raising Exceptions, 189

Random Integers, 15

Random Module, 15

Random Numbers, 15

Random Seed, 280

Raw Strings, 65

Read() Method, 144

Reading CSV Files, 150

Reading Files, 143

Readline() Method, 144

Read-Only, 254

Recursive Functions, 128

Relational Operators, 27

Relative Import, 139

Reloading Modules, 137

Remove, 78

Remove() Method, 79

Removing Elements, 275

Rename File, 153

Repetitions, 54, 55

Requests, 208

Reshaping A Numpy Array, 281

Returning Values, 123

Reusability, 135

Right Operand, 24

Run Migrations, 315

S

Scientific Notation, 14

Select() Method, 222

Selecting Columns, 287

Selecting Rows, 288

Sending Files, 213

Sequence, 6, 7, 17, 47

Series, 283

Server Loads, 228

Sessions, 214

Set, 111

Set Comprehension, 117

Setdefault, 107

Sets, 17, 111

Setter Method, 252

Settings.Py, 309

Shape, 270

Sibling, 226

Simple Iteration, 118

Simulations, 15

Single Forward Slash, 22

Single Inheritance, 170

Size, 271

Slicing, 55, 57, 75

Slicing Arrays, 273

Sort() Method, 79

Sorting A List, 79

Sorting Arrays, 276

Sorting Data, 292

Specific Exceptions, 187

Square Bracket, 73, 132

Standard Library Module, 137

Statistical Models, 15

Strings, 6, 14, 17, 54, 73

Sub-Expression, 25

Subtraction, 22, 26

Supply, 19

Symbol, 16, 21

Symmetric Difference, 116

Syntax, 16

T

Tags, 221

Tasks, 200, 203

Templateview, 321

TESTING, 192

Tests, 61

Text Attribute, 223

Textual Data, 16

The Range() Function, 48

Thread Synchronization, 239

Timeouts, 216

Triple Quotes, 61

True, 28

True And False, 17

Trunc() Function, 13

Try-Except Block, 185

Tuple(), 95

Tuples, 6, 16, 17, 90

Type, 271

U

Union of Two Sets, 114

Unit Testing, 193

Unittest Module, 194

Unpacking, 91

Update() Method, 108

Updateview, 321

URL Configurations, 323

Urls.Py, 310

User Defined Exceptions, 190

V

Validating User Inputs, 256

Validation Logic, 260

Value, 12, 16

Valueerror, 187

Values, 16, 17, 21, 98

Values() Method, 106

Variable Number, 127

Variables, 17

Various Types Of Control Statements, 41

Verify Your Django Project, 311

Versatile Representation Of, 16

Views.Py, 310

Virtual Environment, 305

Visualizing With Matplotlib, 296

W

Web Development, 303

Web Scraping, 218, 227

Websites, 302

While Loop, 46, 48

Working With CSV Files, 149

Write-Only, 254

Writing CSV Files, 150

Wsgi.Py, 309

Z

Zero, 13

Zip, 86

Zip() Function, 86

www.ingramcontent.com/pod-product-compliance
Lightning Source LLC
LaVergne TN
LVHW081514050326
832903LV00025B/1492